Look Out, World~ I'm Me!

The Collected Best of

Jamie Buckingham

Unless otherwise noted, all Scripture quotations are from the
Holy Bible, New International Version. Copyright © 1973,
1978, 1984, International Bible Society. Used by permission.

Scripture quotations marked AMP are from the Amplified Bible.
Old Testament copyright © 1965, 1987 by the Zondervan
Corporation. The Amplified New Testament copyright © 1954,
1958, 1987 by the Lockman Foundation. Used by permission.

Scripture quotations marked KJV are from
the King James Version of the Bible.

Scripture quotations marked NKJV are from the New King
James Version of the Bible. Copyright © 1979, 1980, 1982
by Thomas Nelson Inc., publishers. Used by permission.

Scripture quotations marked Phillips are from *The
New Testament in Modern English*, Revised Edition.
Copyright © 1958, 1960, 1972 by J.B. Phillips.
Macmillan Publishing Co. Used by permission.

CONTENTS

FOREWORD

FOR A quarter of a century, Jamie Buckingham's words gave shape and substance to the charismatic movement. For the last thirteen of those years, I had the privilege of being the "stuffy editor," as Jamie liked to call me, for his column in *Charisma & Christian Life* magazine.

Originally titled Dry Bones, in 1982 his column was renamed Last Word and ensconced in its now familiar position in the back of the magazine. When his first column ran in March 1979, Jamie's books had sold millions of copies, and he was already a force in the burgeoning charismatic movement.

At that time, *Charisma* was a fledgling magazine with barely fifteen thousand subscribers. A recent graduate of journalism school, I could hardly believe I was editing Jamie Buckingham, someone I considered the greatest Christian writer of our day.

Jamie eventually wrote or ghostwrote forty-seven books that sold a total of more than thirty-four million copies. Yet for all his books and speaking engagements, toward the end of his life he was probably best known for having the Last Word each month. That's because he was at his best when writing a column.

Jamie was a gifted essayist, and the 850-word monthly format was perfect for him. It allowed him to write on a variety of timely topics, commenting on current events and trends in the kingdom.

He also could write about topics that did not lend themselves to being books — about things he held dearest (like his family, his relationship with Wycliffe Bible Translators or his local church) and about things he despised (like pompous preachers, hypocrites and frauds). He could wax eloquent on the meaning of life — or tickle us with stories about toupees or squishy tomatoes or washing machines possessed by sock-gobbling demons.

Because good humor is so rare in Christian circles, Jamie is often best remembered for his wit. In fact, we published a collection of his humorous writings in a book titled *The Truth Will Set You Free, But First It Will Make You Miserable* (Creation House).

Jan Crouch of TBN enjoyed the book so much that she used to read some of the chapters on the air. One time when Jamie was a guest, she read the chapter about how he piously tried to repeat in the second service what the Holy Spirit had supernaturally done in the early service — only to embarrass himself by asking the congregation to "bow your eyes and close your heads."

When Jamie died in February 1992 and TBN ran a tribute to him, they reran a portion of that show. The family liked it so much that they played TBN's tribute at his funeral. It had everyone laughing, which is exactly the way Jamie would have liked it.

Jamie was great at poking holes in people's religious balloons, even if it meant poking fun at himself. Once he confessed that, after telling preachers to stay off secular talk shows, he accepted an invitation to be Geraldo Rivera's guest (see chapter 12).

Not all of Jamie's columns were funny. Many dealt with challenges faced by believers. Some reflected his burden to build bridges between separated brethren or extend a loving hand to hurting people. All of them brought us face-to-face with Jesus.

His column in *Charisma* was so popular that nearly everyone read it first. I think even my own mother skipped my column up front to read Jamie's first. When he died we knew our readers would miss the column, so we decided to run it for at least thirteen issues, reprinting the best column from each year he wrote for *Charisma*.

Since I had edited the columns, I went back through past issues to pick the best one for each year. As I reread them, I was struck by the simple beauty of his writing, by his uncommon insights, by the breadth of the topics he covered. I remembered being baffled about how to edit Jamie. His writing was so good — so much better than mine — that I barely knew where to begin. Usually the columns were printed with few editorial changes.

But a couple of times a year I felt I had to return a column for a rewrite. If for no other reason I needed to remind Jamie — and myself — that I was the editor, the one with the last word about Jamie's Last Word. Besides, believe it or not, Jamie didn't write brilliantly every time. Rather than rewrite that column, he'd usually send in another one much better than the first. And I could count on him to remark at an embarrassing moment (like at a writers' conference) about how I "cruelly rejected" one of his most brilliant pieces of writing.

Of course I didn't really mind. I knew it was all part of the give-and-take relationship we had developed. We were much more than just editor and columnist. Though in many ways he was my mentor, we were colleagues, confidants and friends. Over the years, I gave Jamie great freedom in what he wrote in his Last Word, and he helped me develop my writing and editing skills as *Charisma* grew to be a national publication.

Now he's gone, and I worry about how we will replace his wit and wisdom in *Charisma*. There will never be another Jamie Buckingham. Many others who loved his writings share the loss. Though they never had the opportunity to know him as I did — to journey with him to the top of Mount Sinai or chase him around a racquetball court — they still feel they knew him because he was so personal in his writing.

Many of these readers have written and asked us to print his 153 columns from *Charisma* in a book. To have done so would have required a 480-page book, costing more than twenty dollars. So we have collected sixty-eight of the best, arranged them by subject matter and presented them here for you.

For those of you who read *Charisma*, these stories should prompt a flood of memories for you as they did for me. For other readers who never read the magazine, you will enjoy his insights, his humor and the beauty of his writing for the first time.

Read them and enjoy.

Stephen Strang
Longwood, Florida
November 18, 1992

Part One

On Being Real Men

One

LOOK OUT, WORLD — I'M ME!

I T SEEMS I'm to spend my life paddling upstream. While many of my Christian brothers are happily floating with the current, here I am doggedly battling in the opposite direction.

Some of my friends say I am rebellious. Independent. Unsubmissive.

Not so. I am, however, determined to regain my uniqueness, my individuality, those things that peer pressure seems dedicated to sweep away.

For instance, I am weary of being pushed around by fashion and advertising moguls who not only tell me what to wear but want to turn me into a walking billboard for their products.

So I refuse to wear T-shirts that have "Nike" or "Adidas" emblazoned on the chest.

Last week my wife gave me a dress shirt that had "Pierre Cardin" stitched on the pocket. Obviously she had me confused with an old boyfriend. Since my name is Jamie, not Pierre, I gave it back. Neither, by the way, is my name "Levi" or "Hang Ten."

I'm me!

I tried to make that point at the auto dealership when our new car arrived. It's bad enough wearing a Rabbit sign without being forced to be a rolling advertisement for Honest John's Auto Hut.

So I asked Honest John to remove his little sign from the tailgate. When he showed dismay, I suggested a compromise. I would drive around with his little sign on my car if he would pay me a royalty of two cents per mile in the city and one cent per mile on the highway. That's the way songwriters do it, you know.

He didn't think that was funny — and removed the sign.

I'm not, as a friend accused, a cynic. But I am more than a piece of flotsam being washed along in the current.

All my experiences are unique — even those shared with others. I'm not a sheep to be herded; I'm a saint for whom Christ died. I choose to submit as an act of my will.

But God has not called me to unscrew my head and store my intellect in a jar. Nor am I simply to put my brain in neutral and buzz with the swarm.

His Spirit has sanctified my intellect as well as my emotions. Not only am I free in the spirit, but also I am free to think.

I detest crowds. I stay home on July 4 and go to the beach when I can walk alone on the sand. The idea of being part of a crowd of a million people at a religious rally horrifies me. I'd much rather be alone in the woods with God — or sitting in a quiet restaurant with friends.

I value and protect my individuality — my uniqueness. It is the essence of being, the mark of creation, the reason for redemption. Christ did not die to make us robots but to restore us to personhood.

In my free thinking, however, there are lines I choose not to cross — boundaries defined for me in God's Word. Yet I refuse to be labeled a "fundamentalist" or put in a "liberal" box. I'm not a them — or a they. I'm a me.

The system tried to label Jesus, to give Him a title. That's the way the system controls you. Then you can be classified as a they or a those. Jesus just smiled and said, "If you need a title, call Me 'Son of Man.' "

He, too, was a me. Not a they.

For years I refused to wear a necktie — simply because everyone else did. Then I began to hear things like "Jamie's one of those who never wears a tie."

So I started wearing (on occasion) a three-piece suit with a necktie.

But that's part of the price of swimming upstream. I eat at Fred and Ethel's restaurant rather than at Wendy's. If time allows, I choose the back roads rather than the interstates. I stay in small motels, wear old clothes, cut my own hair, read gutsy books and go to movies of my own choosing. And sometimes I grow a mustache just because I want to.

I'm me.

Last year when a tuxedo-wearing evangelist at a convention announced that everyone in the room was going to be slain in the Spirit as he walked down the aisle, I was the only one who remained standing. My wife accused me — from her prone position under the chairs — of being stubborn, independent and rebellious.

I'm none of these. I'm just me. A unique creature for whom Christ died.

To lay down your individuality is the worst of all blasphemies, for it negates the death of Christ. Your uniqueness is your most precious possession. Don't waste it floating downstream.

Two

A SMALL TRIBUTE

I CAN take you to the exact place, and re-enact the exact scene, where the lights flickered back on in my life.

Twenty of us, from all over the nation, arrived that Sunday afternoon at the huge stone mansion called Wainwright House, located above New York City on Long Island Sound. We were guests of *Guideposts* magazine and had come to attend a week-long writer's workshop.

Norman Vincent Peale, the publisher, and Catherine Marshall, wife of *Guideposts* editor Leonard LeSourd, had planned the workshop. They had asked writers — and writers-to-be — to submit a manuscript. It would be judged, and twenty writers would be selected to attend an all-expense-paid week studying under the magazine's editors.

When I spotted the notice in the magazine, it was like Moses seeing the burning bush. Two years earlier I would have passed it by. But during the last twenty-four months I had been fired from two churches as pastor. The first time was in South Carolina. I had escaped, just one step in front of the T&F Committee (tar and feathers gang), to start over in Florida in another church. There I lasted fifteen months and was fired again.

The second firing was vicious. Deeply wounded, I had since

huddled alone in our rented house with my equally wounded wife and five small children. In shame, I realized my ministerial life was finished. Like Moses, I was doomed to wander in the wilderness.

But what does a man do when all he can do — all he wants to do — is denied him? What does he do when deep within there remains a call to tell people about God — but now he is declared disqualified?

I did the only thing there was to do: I walked through whatever door opened. In this case I submitted a manuscript to *Guideposts*. If no one would listen to my sermons, maybe they would read my stories.

In late September 1967 I received a telegram from LeSourd. (I still have it, framed, on the wall of my writing studio.) Out of many entrants I, along with nineteen others, had been chosen.

So I arrived that Sunday afternoon at Wainwright House to see a burning bush. But I had no hope. My bushes had burned before — and were always consumed.

That night after dinner we gathered in the huge walnut-paneled great room of the old stone mansion. A fire was crackling in the fireplace. Outside the autumn leaves brushed against the leaded glass windows. We sat in easy chairs around the room. Twenty of us. All strangers.

The editors were introduced: John and Elizabeth Sherrill, who had written books I had never read; Catherine Marshall and her husband, Leonard LeSourd. Arthur Gordon, who later replaced LeSourd as editor, was there. So was Van Varner, who succeeded him. But dominating the room was Peale.

I was impressed but struggled with my feelings. For years I had warned others about his writings. I thought of all the times I had stood in my pulpits (before I was fired) and made fun of his positive thinking. Now here I was — his guest.

Jovial, relaxed, he started by saying, "Since I'm paying the bill, I should find out who you are."

We started around the room, introducing ourselves. Everyone present was a professional: Jim Hefley, who had written more books than a man could ever read; Dick Schneider, later to become senior editor of the magazine; Irene Harrell, a top devotional writer. All the others were magazine editors, book authors and newspaper writers.

I had never written anything but sermons.

As they listed their credits, I panicked. What could I say? Surely not the truth. It was almost my turn. I whispered to my neighbor, "You go next. I've got to use the bathroom."

I slipped out of the room, too embarrassed to introduce myself as the failure I was.

I waited behind a velvet curtain near the door until Peale was talking again. Only then did I slip back to my chair. I had never felt so lonely. I wanted to go home, but home was even lonelier.

"No one is here by accident," Peale was saying. "You have each been chosen."

Then (and to this day I believe he looked straight at me) he said, "Not only did our editors choose you. God has chosen you. He has called you to something greater than you've ever dreamed. Tonight is the beginning of something bigger than any of us can imagine."

He said more, but that was all I needed. The lights had flickered back on in my life.

A man can live without faith and love. But no man can survive without hope. That night Norman Vincent Peale gave me hope. My bush was burning.

The next afternoon John Sherrill pulled me aside. A New Jersey publisher, he said, was looking for someone who could write a book. He recommended me. I walked through that door, too, simply because it opened. That was the first of forty-seven books — and the bush burns brightly, still not consumed.

It was Michelangelo who reportedly said of sculpture that "the finished form exists within the uncut stone; the sculptor need only release it." That night Norman Vincent Peale picked up mallet and chisel. Looking across the room at a flawed stone, he struck a gentle blow of hope.

I heard the old sculptor was once again under attack by men such as I used to be. This time he was accused of being part of a worldwide conspiracy to seduce Christianity. I do not need to defend him. God, and history, will do that. I just wanted to write this small tribute and say, "For looking beyond the flawed surface to the finished form within, thank you."

Three

DO REAL
MEN HUG?

IN ONE of his management newsletters, Harry Levinson says, "People benefit from sharing their pain. They find strength in the ability to ask for help, not because they can't do without it, but because mutual support makes both parties stronger, both lives easier and both lives richer."

Women, it seems, have less trouble with this than men. They don't seem to mind asking for help if they need it. Men, on the other hand, resist asking for help. We have been trained by coaches, drill instructors, Boy Scout leaders and big brothers that it's "macho" to stand alone, to be tough, to make it on our own. Only weaklings ask for help. After all, what good does it do to have a college degree, a pilot's license or thirty years' experience if we still have to ask someone to help us?

Take the average man who loses his way driving through a strange city. His wife is beside him, and his mother-in-law is in the back seat. Both women are adamant he should stop and ask directions.

Does he do it?

Not on your life. Gripping the steering wheel with white knuckles and staring straight ahead, he drives and turns and turns and drives, cursing the way the city is laid out and those idiots who never know how to put up a decent road sign. At best he might pull off the road, look at a map and try to figure out where he is. At worst his wife forces him to stop by threatening to jump out of the car. In the end he runs short of gas, and while he is filling the tank his mother-in-law says to the attendant, "My stubborn son-in-law is too proud to ask directions. How do we find...?"

Men don't like to ask for help. Especially from their wives, mothers, mothers-in-law, employees, employers, peers, strangers, friends or other men. Because of this strange concept of masculinity, real men, we are taught, not only do not eat quiche, neither do they ask for help.

Nor do they hug.

It's like shedding tears, kneeling at an altar or saying, "I love you," to another man. We men prefer a strong handshake or at best a hearty clap on the back. That's macho!

I remember the instructions my dad gave to each of the four Buckingham boys as we grew up. (I'm not sure how he handled this with our baby sister.) "Shake hands like a man," he said. "Take the initiative. Grasp the other fellow's hand firmly. Squeeze with gentle strength, shake slightly and look him in the eye. Never look at his forehead, his chin or his mouth. Always in the eye. This way you're in control."

Much later I learned the handshake is the perfect defense against the pusher who wants to invade my "private space" — that eighteen-inch perimeter which forms a sacred aura around my body. All men, and most women, according to psychological studies, set up this perimeter of defense. Like a magnetic field, it is designed to keep folks from getting into our yards and looking into our windows. It stems from a don't-get-close-to-me spirit and causes us to ward off all male huggers (and especially kissers).

A sociologist from North Carolina State University pointed out, "The male twosome is rare and seems designed more for combat than for comfort." For that reason male relationships seldom deepen into intimacy. They stay at the superficial and guarded level, meaning most men treat each other the way two male dogs might as they meet on the sidewalk, politely sniffing, but with the hairs on the back always slightly bristled.

This is sad, for inside every man is a little boy who has never stopped looking for a pal.

Why, then, are we men so reluctant to have close friends, to form relationships, to let our brothers and sisters know where we are hurting and ask for help?

The Bible says the reason is *pride*. It's an awful thing, this pride. It not only prevents us from asking for help and from hugging, but it robs us of deep and lasting relationships.

We men need to learn how to express our need for warmth, security and other deep emotions. We need to learn to lean on our brothers, to put an arm around a hurting friend, to let a friend put his arms around us and help heal our hurts. In short, we need to grow up, stop being afraid some woman is going to ensnare us with a mother's apron string, or some man put us back under a father's tyrannical thumb.

We men need to learn from our female counterparts that it can be comforting and strengthening to admit weakness rather than hiding it. Perhaps we might discover others have weaknesses too, and in the process of our seeking comfort, we can become a comforter.

It's risky, fellows. There is a real danger you might reach out and be misunderstood — or even rejected. I'm not saying this kind of love and honesty is easy, but we have to start somewhere.

Why not with each other?

Four

HOLY KISSING

FEW THINGS traumatize us real men any more than being kissed by another man. I remember vividly the first time it happened to me. The fellow was a transplant into our church from Ohio. Broad and bearded, he came forward after the service to introduce himself. I tried to shake his hand. Instead he kissed me on the cheek.

I could feel my face turning flaming red. I knew I ought to kiss him back. Five times the Bible says we should greet one another with a holy kiss. That's more times than it says we should be born again. But I couldn't. I just couldn't.

It took me weeks to recover. A month later, after doing my best to evade the man on Sunday, he kissed me again. But I simply could not pucker up in return.

Real men, I had been taught from childhood, don't kiss other men. They shake hands.

It was tough enough just learning how to hug.

I got my first exposure to hugging in 1967 at a Full Gospel Business Men's Fellowship convention in Washington, D.C. It was horrible, crammed into that hotel lobby with four thousand hugging charismatics.

Two things stood out about that group. First, they were a people who vocalized their affection to God with unabashed shouting — even in public places. Second, they showed their affection to each other — by hugging. It was as if all charismatics had adopted a slogan: "No handshaking allowed." Even my own father didn't hug me. But these people hugged everyone. And worse, they pounded you on the back at the same time, shouting "Praise God!" to draw attention to their bizarre behavior.

Eventually, in self-defense, I too became a hugger. It was easier to throw my arms around everyone than it was to try to determine who was a handshaker and who was a hugger.

Then I ran across those verses about holy kissing.

I did everything I could to escape it. I checked all the different Bible translations, only to discover the Bible translators were as inhibited as I.

Kenneth Taylor, from Moody Bible Institute, translated 2 Corinthians 13:12: "Greet each other warmly in the Lord" (TLB).

Clarence Jordan, a Southern Baptist, used a good Baptist phrase: "Extend to one another the hand of fellowship."

And J.B. Phillips, a proper Anglican, gave it a British twist: "A handshake all round, please!"

The Bible translators were tracking the culture rather than translating the Word.

I opened my seldom-used Greek New Testament. In five instances we are told to greet each other with a kiss (Rom. 16:16; 1 Cor. 16:20; 2 Cor. 13:12; 1 Thess. 5:26; 1 Pet. 5:14).

For centuries men have tried to get around this. In A.D. 1250 the Anglicans introduced the Pax (peace) Board so they could pass the "kiss of peace" without moral contamination. The clergy kissed the board then passed it to the congregation, who in turn kissed it. The idea didn't last long. One sick priest could wipe out his entire congregation.

The Puritans — while allowing the kiss — translated "holy" to mean men should kiss men and women should kiss women. To enforce this they separated the men from the women in the church house, sometimes with a partition down the middle.

In our day, besides all the cultural and traditional hang-ups we have to overcome, holy kissing is said to encourage weirdos, child molesters and dirty old men.

"That's all my fornicating husband is looking for — a scriptural excuse," one angry wife told me after hearing a sermon on biblical kissing.

And what about the weirdos? My teenage daughters used to come home and talk about "that man" in the church. (Every church has its "that man.") "Daddy, that man hugs all the girls with a funny hug."

My reply: "When he does, rub your lipstick all over his shirt. Then let his wife straighten him out."

One stern-faced man warned me that kissing — like dancing, women wearing slacks and "mixed swimming" — would soon lead to sexual orgies, wife-swapping and child molestation.

But I'm tired of letting the devil steal all the good stuff. A holy kiss comes from a holy heart. We live in a loveless world. So many are never hugged, never kissed. Love is relegated to sex and silly greeting cards. How desperately we need to give — and receive — affection.

So watch out. The next time you see me, you just might get kissed.

Five

MY STATEMENTS DON'T CARRY AS MUCH WEIGHT AS THEY USED TO

FOR YEARS I've watched my fat friends lose weight then condemn the rest of us fatties for not being as spiritual as they are.

A couple of years ago the bookstores were glutted (appropriate word) with books on how to lose weight. Unfortunately, many of the people who wrote those books are now fat again.

That makes for a poor witness.

Several years ago I lost fifteen pounds on a fast. I immediately went into the pulpit and "called the body to slimness."

A lot of fat people left the church.

Not to be outdone, I wrote an infamous magazine column which I illustrated with a specially designed suit of armor for fat people over the caption "Put on the whole armor of God."

More criticism — this time from folks saying I was making fun of pregnant women and people with glandular problems.

In retaliation for their criticism I went out and ate a lot of ice cream — and gained twenty-five pounds.

For twenty-six years I had been fat. However, with all my huffing and puffing when I climbed stairs, and my bulging eyeballs every time I bent over to tie my shoes, I knew there was something inherently sinful about being overweight.

To be fat in a world that is starving to death is inconsistent with the attitude of Jesus.

Yet nothing — no amount of fasting — seemed to change my shape or weight.

While my body was supposed to be the temple of the Holy Spirit, I had turned it into a cathedral — complete with flying buttresses and expansive porticos.

Then our home church — the small group to whom I relate and submit — (most of whom were overweight and some of whom were fat) decided it was time to get in shape. We began bringing a set of bathroom scales to our Monday night meetings. One night we even took the scales to the Chinese restaurant when we went out to eat as a group. We fined ourselves huge amounts of money for each pound gained.

At the end of the period I was not only fatter, I was poorer.

One morning in June I got up and looked in the mirror. My face was puffy. My eyelids drooped. I needed a brassiere, and my tummy was so big I couldn't see my knees.

To sum it up, I was dying. Perhaps, more accurately, being crushed to death.

How could this be since just a few months before I felt I had heard God say He would give me another fifty years of productive life?

I found myself studying a verse of Scripture in Exodus 15. God had told the Israelites, "I will not bring on you any of the diseases I brought on the Egyptians, for I am the Lord, who heals you" (v. 26b).

I needed a healing. But that promise, like most of God's promises, was in the subjunctive mood. It was preceded by certain conditions before it was valid. "Listen carefully to the voice of the Lord your God and do what is right in his eyes...pay attention to his commands and keep all his decrees" (Ex. 15:26a).

God had told me a long time ago to lose weight. Now, because I had disobeyed, I had become the American version of an Egyptian fleshpot.

"I am the Lord who heals you" does not apply to those who are deliberately self-indulgent. Butter-soaked waffles for breakfast and strawberry shortcake before going to bed will bring on the plagues of Egypt just as quickly as the disobedience of a stiff-necked pharaoh.

As I examined my false starts into slimness across the years, I realized my failures stemmed from wrong motives. I wanted to look good, wanted to brag, wanted to lord it over fat folks, wanted to impress people, wanted to live longer. All were insufficient motives.

There is only one valid motive: the desire to please God through obedience.

In June I put a chart on the door of my refrigerator and ran a line from my weight of 215 to my goal of 170.

I had never been on a diet before, having lost weight the "macho" way by fasting. Our daughter-in-law was a distributor for a diet plan, and my wife and I decided we'd go on the diet together.

The result was a weight loss of forty-five pounds in ninety days.

During that time I totally changed my eating habits. I am determined never, never, never to return to where I was.

What are the secrets for my success?

- I did it "unto the Lord," and for no other reason.
- I made losing weight my top priority. Jackie and I put the scales in the front foyer of our house. I weighed myself every morning as soon as I got out of bed and marked my progress on the chart.
- Jackie and I did it together. (She lost twenty-six pounds.) That meant we could encourage — and badger — each other.
- Our home church cooperated, not with all those wild concepts as before, but by everyone determining God was calling us to a radical change of life-style.
- As soon as I reached my goal, I had my clothes taken up, giving away those too big to re-fit. It had the effect of burned bridges. I cannot go back to being fat. It would cost too much.
- God said I could not talk about my weight loss for six months — until I had proved I could keep it off.

The time is now up. I weigh in at 171. That's ten pounds less than when I graduated from high school. And while I know better than to brag, it sure feels good to rise in the morning, flex in front of the mirror and wink at myself.

Even though my statements don't carry as much weight as they used to, they come forth with a lot more conviction. It feels good to obey.

Six

BREAKING
BARRIERS

ALTHOUGH I never placed better than third in any track meet, I spent a lot of time in college practicing the shot put.

In my sophomore year an Irish American by the name of Pat O'Brien won a gold medal in the Olympics by throwing the sixteen-pound iron ball fifty-seven feet. It was a new world record. Experts said O'Brien might be able to do a few inches better if he practiced, but no one would ever be able to break the sixty-foot barrier.

But Pat O'Brien began experimenting with different styles. Instead of hopping across the ring, he began to spin, like the discus throwers. Four years later he won the Olympics again — and broke the unbreakable barrier by tossing the shot sixty feet, eleven inches.

From that time on every shot-putter worth his salt has gone beyond sixty feet. In the 1980 Olympics a Russian threw the shot seventy feet, and the world record was set by Udo Beyer of East Germany with seventy-two feet, eight inches.

With each successive Olympics, someone is sure to throw it even farther.

All because one man broke through.

Remember the four-minute mile barrier? No one, the experts said, would ever be able to run the mile in less than four minutes.

Then in 1954 a young medical student by the name of Roger Bannister did the impossible. He broke the barrier.

Today every world-class runner on the circuit can run the mile in less than four minutes. In fact, Sebastian Coe ran the mile in three minutes and forty-seven seconds — thirteen seconds less than the impossible.

All because one man broke through.

When I was in college, the experts said no one would ever be able to break the impossible barrier of fifteen feet in the pole vault. At that time the Rev. Bob Richards held the record at 14 feet, 11 1/2 inches. Then an enterprising young athlete began experimenting with a fiberglass pole and soared over the impossible barrier. A record was established by a young Polish athlete who jumped 18 feet, 11 1/2 inches. That's eight feet higher than Irving Baxter jumped when he won the 1900 Olympics.

During the next Olympics there is a good chance someone will go beyond the twenty-foot mark — *all because one man broke through.* [Editor's note: In 1991, seven years after this article was written, Sergei Bubka jumped 20 feet, 1/4 inch.]

That same Irving Baxter, by the way, won the 1900 Olympics with a high jump of six feet, two inches. For years the experts said the impossible barrier in the high jump was seven feet. Then a young man by the name of Fosbury said, "You guys are jumping wrong. Instead of throwing one leg over the bar first, you need to jump over the bar backward — headfirst." Critics called his unorthodox style the Fosbury Flop. But he broke the impossible barrier, and a new record was made by an East German at 7 feet, 8 3/4 inches.

All because one man broke through.

Breaking through is part of life. Jesus said, "The kingdom of heaven has been forcefully advancing, and forceful men lay hold of it" (Matt. 11:12). In other words, the kingdom of heaven belongs to those who break through.

When God told Joshua the promised land was his, it meant it was his to TAKE. Every place he set his foot belonged to him, God said. The problem was that the land was occupied. In order to put his foot down, he had to move someone else's boot. By force.

Desiring a thing is not enough. You have to go after it. That takes commitment. And discipline.

I discovered this when I lost all that weight. Simply wanting to be thin was not sufficient. Even positive confession wouldn't accomplish my desire. I had to fight for thinness — one pound at a time. Even after achieving my goal three months later I still had (and have) to fight to maintain it. That which I have taken from the devil by force, I now understand, he would like to reclaim through chocolate ice cream.

No spiritual victory has come easy. With each one I have had to overcome someone who said, "It can't be done."

This is true in my struggle to break through to holiness, in my battle to bring my marriage to the place of perfect unity, in my fight to overcome selfishness and fear. "You'll always be the way you are," the experts say.

But like O'Brien, Bannister, Fosbury and the rest, I am determined to break through.

It can be done. At Calvary Jesus broke the impossible barrier. He opened the door for all the rest of us to follow. Now in the power of His Spirit I can say: Once a man is satisfied he is in the center of God's plan and that God is working out His plan through him, that man is invincible.

All because a Man broke through.

Part Two

—

ON THE ART OF
FAMILY LIFE

Seven

A Dad Remembers and Rejoices

DEAR BONNIE:
Your call from Tulsa, telling us that you are expecting your first baby, has filled the old home place with joy.

Your mom — and your brothers and sisters — are ecstatic. You could tell, of course, when Robin grabbed the phone and started squealing. I believe she's more excited over your "good news" than over the birth of her own children.

What do I feel?

Well, while the rest of the family is back in the kitchen celebrating, I have withdrawn to my quiet place back here in my study to think — and remember.

I'm proud of you and Marion. During your two years of marriage you have proved yourselves hard workers and able managers. Marion has a great future ahead, and you are already an outstanding artist and illustrator.

Thus when you announced several months ago that you wanted to have a baby, I knew it would cost you something. Choosing a baby over a career is a difficult decision. You and Marion are earning good salaries. That will be chopped in half when you stop working — while your expenses will increase.

But yours is the finer decision. Your mom and I are proud you have chosen a baby over money.

There are, in the lives of most women, three significant times. They are menstruation, marriage and childbirth.

The first time begins at the marvelous moment when a girl's body announces she is no longer a child but has become a woman.

For some girls this is terrifying. They have not been taught that their bodies are fearfully and wonderfully made. They do not know that the sign of blood is not a signal of death, but the heralding of a new age — that the menstrual cycle is not a curse but the signal that her body is now capable of bearing new life.

I realize, as a man, I've never had to go through the monthly bloating and cramping caused by the menstrual period. I remember vividly all those times during your teen years when I would hear you moaning in the night. I would go into your room and spend long hours sitting on the side of your bed, rubbing your back and praying.

I suffered with you, sweetheart. I know it was painful. The missed days of school. The times of aloneness, hurting upstairs in your bedroom or lying on the sofa with a heating pad.

Not all women suffer as severely. But you, and your mom, know the agony of such pain.

I was first exposed to all this when your mom and I were dating back in high school. I knew almost nothing of female anatomy and could not understand her monthly cramps.

I remember a long trip home from college our sophomore Thanksgiving. We were in the back seat of a friend's car, traveling through southern Georgia and northern Florida. Your mom, who was then wearing my engagement ring, was in severe pain. She lay across my lap, moaning, while I rubbed her back and felt totally helpless. It seems I've been rubbing backs ever since — hers, yours and your two sisters'.

But out of those times of agony your mom gave birth to five wonderful children who have all grown up to love the Lord and honor their parents. You were the third conception. You are the product of her pain — not only in childbirth, but also in those earlier years as she got ready.

Now, sweetheart, you too are pregnant. You and Marion, in love, have joined together to create another life. There will be more pain as the baby is born, but it will all be forgotten in the glory of the miracle.

Thus the other two stages of woman's life are inexorably bound to that first significant event of emerging adolescence. They are the times for which every woman is created — marriage and childbirth. Even though a woman may never marry, or marries and remains childless, the yearning to mate and reproduce remains. And many confess they feel less than complete until these moments are achieved.

You, though, have been blessed with a wonderful, loving, God-fearing husband. Now you are blessed with pregnancy — the time when a woman achieves her greatest physical beauty. From the time you were conceived to this pending moment of birth, God has been preparing you to create new life.

That is the reason you are such a fine artist. You love to take nothing and turn it into something beautiful. That is what you and Marion have done. You have taken common sperm and ordinary egg and put them together in love. The result is the new life which grows in your belly.

It is a marvelous picture, Bonnie, of what Christ has done for us. The blood of Jesus is the central issue of our salvation. Some look upon blood as ugly, but it is the blood which makes us capable of reproducing.

Ahead of you lies the greatest fulfillment of human experience. Although the male is spared the pain of the menstrual cycle, yet he is also denied the honor of creating new life in his body — and the ultimate joy of giving birth to a living child. And one day, as Christ gave us the mighty Holy Spirit, out of your inner being will flow new life.

Your mom and I are immensely happy for you. The fact that we already have three wonderful grandchildren does not diminish our joy. For you are a special person. You are God's gift to us. And now you will bear God's gift to you and Marion.

So the old home place is filled today with rejoicing. I too am proud. These tears, which you cannot see, are tears of nostalgia. But your mom and I renew our covenant with you, to pray for you and the new life growing in you, and to stand with you as you take this next wonderful step toward spiritual fulfillment.

After all, that's what parents — and grandparents — are for.

Lovingly,
Dad

Eight

CHILD REARING: A REMEMBERED ART

O NE AFFLICTION common among grandparents is the urge to take over. I've watched my mother, who is eighty-five, do this to our children. Now, as my own five children grow up, marry and start having children of their own, I find myself doing the same thing. In fact, it's hard to keep from taking over when you know you can do it better — and with my grandchildren I am no exception.

"You don't have to make that mistake," I want to tell my children as they stumble clumsily through child rearing. "Your mom and I have already walked that path. It goes nowhere. Go this way instead."

It seems so simple. All they have to do is follow my advice and they'll rear perfect children. Yet, it may be that real maturity comes only by making mistakes and then having to find a way out of the corner into which you've painted yourself. Reflecting over the years, there are certain things I would do differently if I had the option of starting over. There are other things we did right — things which have really paid off.

I wish, for instance, I had taught my children correct eating habits. I'm not talking about table manners, for we spent a lot of time on that. Rather I am concerned that we raised an entire generation on junk food — ice cream and french fries. Now that Jackie and I have been convicted of our poor eating habits and are making drastic changes (no more white sugar and white bread, few red meats, lots of vegetables, fruits and grains), we find it painful to see our grandchildren eating the same things our children ate.

I wish we had observed a weekly day for family fasting and prayer. I wish we had eaten a family breakfast together with a time for prayer before the children had left for school. I wish we had insisted that each child memorize passages of Scripture.

I wish we had taught each child to save money on a regular basis — setting aside a certain amount each week from allowances and wages. I wish we had read the classics out loud as my dad did to me. I still remember "You're a better man than I am, Gunga Din" and "Build thee more stately mansions, O my soul," not to mention long passages from Shakespeare, Thoreau, Melville and Longfellow. I wish we had listened to classical music as a family. Too often I withdrew to my own room to listen to Chopin and Dvorak rather than insult my ears with the weirdness and wildness coming from the children's radio or phonograph.

But all that is offset by the things we did right. I am glad we led each child to make a personal commitment to Jesus Christ — and that each one has received the baptism in the Holy Spirit. I am glad we taught each child the privilege of tithing as the basis of kingdom stewardship. It's tough watching my married children who make very little money set aside 10 percent of each week's wages for the Lord. But it's also satisfying, for I know the end results.

I'm especially glad for those individual evening prayer times. Each night I would make the rounds, sitting on the side of each child's bed, talking about personal things. Regardless of how tough the day had been, I wanted those last moments of conscious thought to be positive. I wanted each child to know his dad loved him and was proud of him. I did this every night, laying on hands and praying in the Spirit, even if the child was asleep. It was one of my better decisions.

I am glad I honored my own father and mother, and that through that example my children now honor me and their mom. I never called my parents by their first names nor referred to my dad as "the old man." Even though my parents made many mistakes, my dad was always my hero. It is fulfilling to know my own children view me in the same perspective.

Jackie and I have made a lot of mistakes rearing our children. We've done things I wish we hadn't done — like fight in front of them. But we've never held anything back. No subject was taboo in our home. We discussed sex as openly as we discussed why they should wear a shirt at the table and why they should go to church with the family on Sunday.

Perhaps it has been this transparency — this willingness to admit we have been imperfect parents, this open admission that their parents were desperately in need of a Savior — which has knitted us together in such a tightly woven blanket. Now, instead of fleeing from home, all of our grown children have said they want to come back and live close by, along with the grandchildren.

Undoubtedly, that's going to cost me some money. After all, grandchildren need shoes — and some ice cream and french fries now and then, too.

Nine

HOTHEADS IN
THE HOUSEHOLD

I NEVER heard my father and mother argue. I now know they often disagreed. But they considered it bad breeding to argue in front of their children.

It was an unreal world for a kid to grow up in.

There was one time...I was about ten years old. I woke in the middle of the night and heard my mother screaming. My older brother, Walter Jr., had come in late from a Saturday night date. My mother met him downstairs, and there was some kind of horrible confrontation.

My mother was hysterical. Her words were shrill. Unintelligible. Then I heard Walter shouting something — also unintelligible. The door slammed, shaking the entire house.

By that time I was out of bed. From my upstairs window I saw my brother stomping across the dark yard toward nowhere, shouting back at the house. My mother, back upstairs, was still hysterical.

I was terrified and crawled back into bed, wishing it had never happened. Through the closed bedroom door I could hear my father's calming voice: "Now, now, he'll be back."

The next morning we all gathered as usual at the breakfast table before leaving for Sunday school. Each child, including Walter, was present. Mother was bustling back and forth from the kitchen, bringing in the Cream of Wheat in the big brown serving bowl with the blue stripe around the top. My father, sitting at the head of the table in coat and tie, had us bow for the blessing. No mention was made of the catastrophic eruption of the night before. In fact, to my knowledge, this is the first time it has ever been mentioned by anyone in fifty years.

But you have to understand, in our family, children were never exposed to their parents' flaws.

My children, unfortunately, were not raised in this kind of artificiality. When Jackie and I argued it seemed to be in front of everyone. That was not the way I would have chosen. I prefer to think of myself as an aristocrat rather than a common brawler. But for some reason or another nothing in our house was private. When it came to our frequent, and sometimes explosive, disagreements, well, everyone knew everything.

My father (and my mother, except for that uncontrollable outburst) regarded unbridled emotion of any kind as bad form. It was suggestive of a lack of Christian restraint. My wife, on the other hand, was one who believed in total exposure. No waiting until the children were asleep. No smiling nicely until we were behind closed doors. Whenever I, by some unacceptable behavior, pushed her over her narrow threshold into the pit of frustration, she simply exploded. Right then.

Earlier in our marriage I was horrified by these outbursts. I wanted my children to think I was perfect. Husbands and wives who shouted at each other in front of their offspring were, in my opinion, products of low breeding. Whenever I found myself in one of these domestic disagreements — and knew the children were listening in — that old terror would return. It was the same feeling I had the night I heard my mother screaming at my brother.

But Jackie did not bring these same fears into our marriage. She had not been raised in a home where domestic disagreements were hidden, where children were lied to by well-meaning parents who attempted to shield them from reality. She was raised in a four-room house occupied by seven people from three generations. Family squabbles involved everyone. She did not fear reality. She knew love would conquer in the end.

Don't misunderstand. I'm not saying it's good for parents to fight in front of their children. Some restraint is good. Any behavior which undermines the foundations of the Christian home is simply unacceptable. But to live lives of polite smiles, lives which deny that last night's nightmare really happened, lives which are designed to hide from children (and others) the reality of disagreements, is the worst kind of hypocrisy.

Across the years, thanks to our growing relationship with God, our household has become more peaceful. We simply don't fight as we used to. Love, joy, peace, gentleness...these have replaced the sharp words and argumentative spirits of our earlier years. We've learned to listen. And respect. Yet if I had to choose between the way of open arguments and the way of my parents, I would choose our way. Our arguments did have one redeeming feature. Once the storm had passed, we knew God required that we make an explanation to our children. It was not unusual to wind up asking the children to pray for us.

Thus our children have never harbored false expectations about their parents or about marriage. They've known from infancy that Mom and Dad not only disagreed but sometimes disagreed violently. They've seen us at our worst: teeth gritted, eyes bulging, voices shouting. They've seen me on my knees sheepishly picking up pieces of a broken bowl I had slammed against the floor. They've seen us both on our knees, before God, confessing and asking forgiveness. The bottom line: They know Mom and Dad simply can't make it without Jesus. As a result, each child has opted to trust Him also.

The five children, now grown and married, often get together at our house for a meal. When they do, the conversation invariably drifts to: "Hey, remember the time Mom...." "Yeah, and what about the time Dad...." This will be followed by hilarious laughter as they explain to their spouses our flaws and faults.

It's embarrassing. But when I hear their laughter and see my wife wink at me, I, too, smile — and give thanks.

Ten

GREATNESS

A S AN entering graduate student at Ft. Worth's Southwestern Baptist Theological Seminary in 1954, I had virtually no concept of what the term "greatness" meant.

I knew there were "great" preachers. These were, I was told,
the magnificent orators, the well-known evangelists and the pastors of large churches.

I knew there were "great" singers. They were, back then, the
soloists who had cut records or had been asked by Billy Graham
to sing at one of his crusades.

But greatness?

As a freshman theologue, with a great disdain for anything
religious, I suspected greatness was in no way related to great —
as in great preacher — just as I suspected quality had little to do
with quantity.

I had never been in the presence of greatness, but I imagined
that if that ever happened I would recognize it by feel rather than
statistic. I also suspected it was rare. Very rare.

My first experience with it came while sitting in the third row
of Ethics 203. The class was taught by T. B. Maston, chairman of
the Christian ethics department.

Ethics, the catalog said, was the study of moral principles and values. It involved the principles of conduct governing an individual or group.

I was interested, but not excited. A cynic, I had never known anyone who seemed to be able — or who really wanted — to live up to the standard they set for others.

Sitting in that class, however, I began to feel there was something about this rather frail, gray-haired professor which rang true.

I had signed up because I wanted to sit under someone who was doing something, rather than just talking about it. Maston was a pioneer in the field of race relations among a people, and in a region where the burning cross was often seen as synonymous with true doctrine. A quiet scholar, he was also a bold reformer, using his pen as a sword to slay the dragons of racial inequality, religious bigotry and injustice against the poor. But what I felt about this man went much deeper than what I knew. He was different.

It was a year before I discovered his wellspring. Others on campus who already knew had seemed too threatened to talk about it. The man who hears a higher call and walks it out among people of lower values is always a threat. But one day I stopped by his house to check an assignment. In the front room I met his then twenty-eight-year-old son, who was totally disabled. The Mastons, because of values, had chosen to raise him rather than put him in an institution.

Ex ungue leonem, the Latins said: "From the claw we may judge the lion." From the part we discover the whole.

Most of the people I knew preached ethics to others. The fact that this great scholar and reformer lived it quietly with his handicapped son awed me.

Across the years my appreciation grew stronger. Even after I was no longer a Southern Baptist I applauded him from afar as he led the fight in race relations. He was constantly on the point, hated by some, admired by others. Year after year he raised the banner of biblical scholarship against legalized gambling, pornography, loose morality and beverage alcohol. He warned us not to repeat the horrible lessons of history in the areas of church and state and religious bigotry. Ethics!

In 1986 T. B. Maston's son, Thomas McDonald Maston, sixty-one, died of cancer.

Tom Mc, as he was called by the few who dared know him, had been born with cerebral palsy. He had never spoken a word. He needed assistance with every bodily function.

Every day for sixty-one years Maston and his wife, Essie, dressed him, fed him, cleaned him, put him to bed and got him out of bed. Tom Mc never brushed his teeth, never tied his shoes, never combed his hair, never raised the lid of a toilet seat. He could not talk. His only means of communication were two simple symbols meaning "yes" and "no."

Yet to the Mastons, Tom Mc was a person of inestimable worth. Ethics!

Early in life the Mastons made a decision they would not "put him away." He was their son, a gift from God, a gift not to be denied.

Essie Maston, a brilliant woman who had the ability to succeed in almost any profession she chose, devoted her entire adult life to caring for her invalid manchild. She deliberately gave up a teaching career rather than hire another to take on the care and parental responsibilities God had given her.

It is impossible for me to comprehend spending my life serving an adult child who had to be fed every bite of food for sixty-one years. I'm too busy bringing in the kingdom, straightening out other people's lives, making certain everyone believes as I do. Values!

Could I value my invalid manchild as more important than I am? A child whose only contribution was to look out at me daily through the glazed windows of his eyes, asking, "Why? Why me, Dad?"

Yet T. B. Maston, believing ethics had to be lived before they could be taught, said nothing was more important than helping his son live out the role God had given him to play. Ethics!

I still can't pinpoint with words what greatness is. But I do know that when I think of it, I think of T. B. and Essie Maston — and their sixty-one years of living love.

Part Three

———

ON THE MEDIA —
GOOD OR BAD NEWS?

Eleven

FREE FROM
THE PRESS

THE MORNING after a recent televangelist scandal broke, I woke to the inner words "Beware of the tumblebugs." It's been a long time since I thought of tumblebugs. Lying in bed, I remembered kneeling as a child in our barnyard watching those little beetles at work. A tumblebug finds a pile of manure. With its front claws it pulls out a small amount, mixes it liberally with beetle spit, works it into a ball, then rolls it across the barnyard — pushing it with its nose.

As I look out over the kingdom I realize God has given His church a huge dose of laxative. The secular media — the tumblebugs of society — smelling the results of God's purgative, have rushed out from under the rocks. They're not looking for the hand of God, much less the face of God. They're not even interested in the type of purgative administered by the Holy Spirit to cleanse and purify His church. All they are nosing for is expelled waste. Once found — and God's people never have been good at digging latrines — they roll it into a neat little TV spot and serve it up on the six o'clock news.

The tragedy is, we bite into it.

No one is a stronger proponent of freedom of the press than I. But it is truth which makes us free, not twisted, slanted, one-sided, incomplete facts. Such stories put us in more bondage than any journalistic censorship imposed by government regulations. A free press in the hands of irresponsible journalists is as dangerous as a vindictive man who shouts "Fire!" in a public theater. The journalists whose primary intent is to catch people in wrongdoing (or who edit film to create the impression of wrongdoing) are instruments of the devil.

Why does the press continually ask questions of Pat Robertson to try to set him up to look like a Pentecostal buffoon?

Remember what the media did to former Secretary of Interior James Watt? Once the newspapers discovered he believed in the return of Christ, they twisted it to mean Watt felt it was OK to destroy our natural resources since the world would be burned up when Jesus returned anyway — the exact opposite of what the secretary believed.

Following my brief foray into the world of the secular media during the PTL scandal, I quickly realized that no good can come from Christians being interviewed on programs such as "Larry King Live," "Nightline" or "60 Minutes." Yet, following the most recent scandal, I saw publicity-hunting preachers by the score drooling to have their pious faces making nonsensical statements on the tube.

Please, please, I said to my friends, don't go on public TV. Your words will be twisted. Let God do His work without your opinions or interference. But it's hard to say no when ABC is on the phone saying the world is waiting for your wisdom.

When will we realize the world does not understand our terminology, our values, our commitment to walk to the sound of a different drummer? Yet we go on public TV and toss out terms even we don't fully understand — terms such as repentance, forgiveness and discipline.

Please, my brothers, shut up and stay home. Talk theology among yourselves. If you go on public TV, talk about God's love.

Remember, dear reader, today's free press is not really free. The facts — especially slanted facts — do not make us free. Only the truth makes us free. Until the press begins reporting on what God is doing, rather than what man is doing (or man's angry or confused reactions to what God is doing), it is never qualified to claim to be free.

Why didn't the free press headline the evangelist's outstanding overseas crusades — the largest in history — as well as his sin?

Why doesn't the free press, in its ninety-seconds-a-night report on the problems in Israel, also remind us that the Koran promises Moslems who kill Jews and Christians a place in heaven?

And would you expect to read in the papers any account of spiritual changes the televangelists might have undergone since their fall?

Like tumblebugs, the media are only interested in something that stinks.

A survey of the Anti-Defamation League found that 51 percent of American Jews thought Israel was responding "too harshly" to the Palestinian rioters. Where did the ADL, Israel's greatest American friend, get its information? From the slanted news served up by the TV tumblebugs.

A *U.S. News and World Report* survey says half the country thinks Pat Robertson is a "religious weirdo" who "scares people." Where does America get its information on Robertson's theology? From the media tumblebugs.

On the basis of a single column in *USA Today* or a horrible picture in the *National Enquirer*, we draw mind-shutting conclusions.

Jesus did not tell Peter, "Blessed are you, Simon Bar-jona, for Dan Rather has revealed this unto you." He said His church was to be built on knowledge from God. Since media revelation is earthly, I'll have to look elsewhere to find what God is saying. It's time for Christians to turn off their TV sets and open their Bibles. Where else can you find a true word on Israel or politics or how to treat a fallen preacher?

Twelve

CONFESSIONS OF A HYPOCRITE

RECENTLY I'VE been praying, asking God about my gifts and calling. Then one morning it came to me very clearly that I had the unique gift of being a hypocrite.

That disturbed me, for I've always looked on hypocrites as preachers who said one thing but did another, or common folks on whom the roofs of the churches fell if they walked into them on any day except Easter.

Actors. That's what the word means, you know. People behind masks. Preachers who wear hairpieces, evangelists who own Busch Beer stock, deacons who keep company with prostitutes.

Actually, though, hypocrites occupy a very important place in the kingdom — like germs and mold. Just look at how many there are. In fact, I seldom go through a day without talking to at least one.

"Your church is full of hypocrites," people complain.

"Then join us. You'll feel right at home," I say.

Actually, we're not as rare as you might imagine. In fact, there are so many of us that most larger churches now have a hypocrites' pastor, just as they have a singles' pastor or youth director.

Since this discovery I've felt a lot better about myself. As it takes one alcoholic to minister to another, my hypocrisy makes me credible when I minister to other hypocrites.

"You are what you hate — you hate what you are," my friend Swen Oleson says. Only he says it with a Swedish accent that makes it sound really profound. The way to discern your gift is to look at your fruit. So I've been doing some fruit inspecting. Sure enough, just as some are apostles, prophets or evangelists — I'm gifted as a hypocrite.

Take this column. Only a genuine hypocrite like me would write a column to Christians saying, "Shut up and stay home. If you go on public TV, talk about God's love," then, before the ink is dry, accept an invitation from Geraldo Rivera to appear on his New York talk show.

"It's Holy Week, and we want you to talk about God's love toward all people," he lied before the show, "especially those who fail."

I should have known right then where the program was headed. But hypocrites are naive. I didn't know until cameras were rolling and they opened with the Swaggart tapes that I had been set up as a tumblebug.

Like most Christians, I have enough religion so that I don't enjoy sinning, but not enough to keep me from it. So, in true hypocritical form, I told the producers I would not answer questions about Swaggart. But instead of walking off the show — as I should have done — I just slouched miserably in my chair while Geraldo played buzzard and went after Swaggart's carcass.

But when I realize one of the reasons I don't do "those things" is that I might get caught, too...well, who's the hypocrite?

Hypocrites are those who don't get caught. Everyone else is just a plain old sinner.

Hypocrites are always afraid one of their old holiness sermons might grow legs and crawl back home. What could be worse than preaching that your sins will find you out, then having one of them find you out?

Hypocrites love to attack other hypocrites. They write nasty letters to editors and sit in television audiences, booing and hissing. One in Geraldo's audience sneered on camera, "We need more Mother Teresas and fewer Tammy Bakkers."

I'd had enough. Despite my resolve to keep my mouth shut, I responded, asking how much money he'd given to Mother Teresa. He got so angry that Geraldo edited out both my question and his vulgar answer.

The really good stuff never makes it on TV — or into print.

When I realized I was gifted as a hypocrite, I was upset. Then I found a verse in the Bible which confirmed it: "For the gifts and calling of God are without repentance" (Rom. 11:29, KJV).

That's me! We hypocrites are "without repentance." But what's there to repent of when you're always right and everyone else is always wrong?

Thirteen

PEACE IN ISRAEL

THE NIGHT before I left Jerusalem there was a riot on the Temple Mount. Fifteen thousand Moslems had gathered inside the forty-acre area surrounding the Mosque of Omar, the huge golden dome which dominates the Jerusalem skyline.

The *mufti*, or Moslem priest, had just finished a hate-filled sermon, calling on all Arab Palestinians to join the *intifada* (Arab word for uprising) and drive the Jews out of the "occupied territories."

Most of the Palestinians who attended the service were not interested in fighting the Israelis. Despite hardships, they know they are thousands of times better off than they were under Arab rule. They returned to their homes peacefully. However, a group of about three hundred young people, ranging in age from ten to twenty, stayed behind, chanting Palestine Liberation Organization slogans. As darkness fell over the Holy City, they picked up rocks — some as big as grapefruits — and began throwing them across the backside of the Western Wall, the Wailing Wall, at peaceful Jewish worshippers.

The Temple Mount police — blue-uniformed Arabs — moved in. Suddenly the youths turned on the police, calling them traitors and Jew-lovers. One young policeman, surrounded by crazed Moslem teenagers, panicked. He fired his gun into the air. Instantly he was struck with a barrage of stones and knocked to the ground, bleeding and unconscious. The youths mercilessly kicked his body, trying to bash his head with stones. The other policemen moved in, firing their guns — loaded with rubber bullets — and throwing tear-gas canisters. When it was over, thirty Arab youths had been wounded and seven policemen were hospitalized.

While all this was going on, American and European TV cameramen — who had been notified earlier of the planned demonstration — filmed merrily away. When the thirty-second stories hit the morning news the next day, they showed Israeli policemen shooting Arab children and hitting them with clubs. No mention was made of the PLO instigators, the *mufti's* sermon or the fact that the policemen were not Jews but Arabs.

Nor was any mention made that the PLO had forced the Arab merchants in Jerusalem and in Bethlehem to close their shops every afternoon to protest Jewish rule of Israel. Since most Jews do not shop in Arab stores, preferring the kosher Jewish shops, the only ones hurt by the strike were the Arabs.

I visited an Arab shop in Jerusalem that I had been to many times before. The night before, it had been burned out by the PLO — in retaliation for the owner's having sold merchandise to tourists on a strike day.

The problem in Israel is not between Jew and Arab. It is between freedom-lovers (Arabs, Jews and Christians) and the PLO, which is backed by Moslem fanatics.

Yet while these isolated instances do occur, the rest of the nation is at peace — another item never reported by the media. Only in the eyes of the press is Israel a war zone. TV sound bites of Israeli soldiers beating Arabs have turned world opinion, including the opinion of many American Jews, against Israel.

There is no easy solution. Arabs in Bethlehem, which is virtually shut down, blame the Jews that there are fifteen thousand Arab college graduates in the area working at menial jobs. What they do not point out is that twenty years ago — under Arab rule — there was no problem. Why? Because there were no colleges. The Israelis who "occupy" the territory have built a number of universities for Arabs. However, Moslem fanatics have prevented the Arabs from building industry to provide jobs. Instead the PLO is constantly calling strikes, intimidating Arab merchants and pulling Arab children out of school to teach them to hate. If only half the Arab oil money spent to supply guns to the PLO was used to build industry in the West Bank, Israeli Arabs would be the most prosperous people on earth.

It's a crazy mentality.

I traveled more than twenty-five hundred miles during my sixteen-day stay — covering the nation. In the Galilee area I stayed on a kibbutz, and I traveled into the Golan Heights and through the high mountains of northern Israel. From there I went to the Dead Sea region, Eilat, and did some mountain climbing in the southern Negev desert. My last days were spent in Jerusalem. At no time did I sense danger. The nation, except for the few hot spots (which are "contained" by the Israeli army), is peaceful — and prospering.

I was there for two reasons. First, to tape more than fifty on-location video devotionals. My nine-member camera crew accompanied me in a minibus.

Second, I was checking out the sites I would walk in September to lead a hiking/teaching tour to out-of-the-way places. I love Israel but will never be satisfied seeing it from a tour bus. The only thing that satisfies is to touch the soil — walk the land.

Israel remains the land of promise, but only God can bring peace.

One afternoon I prayed at the Wailing Wall. The cracks between the stones were filled with slips of paper where people had stuffed written prayers. I removed one and read it. "May the wonderful people of this troubled land, Jew and Arab, find the Messiah — Jesus."

I returned it to its place with an "Amen."

"Pray for the peace of Jerusalem.... May there be peace within your walls and security within your citadels" (Ps. 122:6-7).

Fourteen

EXPECTATIONS

T HE TWO stories were side by side on page 1 of the morning newspaper — both with glaring headlines. One said, "SLAIN PASTOR'S DOUBLE LIFE ALLEGED." The other: "ACCUSED SHOPLIFTER WAS 'GOOD MINISTER.' "

The first story was of an admired Methodist minister in Texas whose body had been found in the back of his van near the town where he pastored. He had been beaten and strangled. The police said there may have been a chance the fifty-five-year-old pastor had been living a double life and was deeply involved in drugs and illicit sex.

That was all the *Dallas Morning News* needed. They waited until Sunday — of course — and ran the article on page 1.

The second story told of a forty-one-year-old Roman Catholic priest in Illinois who along with a sixty-year-old woman was accused of stealing nine thousand dollars' worth of gold jewelry, books, greeting cards and other trivia at a shopping mall. The priest had been arrested Wednesday, but the Chicago papers waited until Sunday to print the story. Our editor printed it alongside the first story in the Monday edition.

Why this obsession on the part of the newspaper editors to give extra publicity to ministers who are accused of going bad?

In fact, anyone claiming to be a Christian runs the risk of newspaper crucifixion if it is discovered he is a sinner.

Several years ago when an elder in our church was accused of mishandling funds in his investment company, the story appeared on page 1 under the head "CHURCH ELDER ACCUSED." His misconduct, though, had absolutely nothing to do with his relationship with our church.

A noted pornographic magazine printed photographs of a deceased congressman, showing him in compromising poses with a prostitute. The pornographer gleefully pointed out that the congressman claimed to be a Christian.

Is this obsession on the part of media people simply a battle of Good against Evil, with Evil doing everything it can to discredit God's people? Or is there something far deeper at work here?

Last year when Lebanese militia sneaked past Jewish guards into a Palestinian refugee camp and murdered hundreds of women and children, the media laid the blame on the Israelis. At the same time, when the Jews did heroic and sacrificial things, the happenings went unreported.

Why does the press love to crucify Jews — and Israeli Jews in particular? Is it merely anti-Semitism, or does it go much deeper?

When you've been persecuted as much as the Jews, it's natural to believe all the world is anti-Semitic. This same syndrome often affects Christians. When a Christian writer recently interviewed a leader of the "discipleship" movement and asked certain questions, the pastor exploded in a violent rage over the phone, accusing the reporter of wanting to "build a case" against his organization. Although his paranoid reaction was understandable (there have been a lot of false accusations in the past), it was unnecessary. The writer was not out to get him, she was just asking honest questions.

It's easy to blame the press. Why don't the media have harsh things to say about the Iranian bloodbath or about the way the Syrians and the Jordanians have treated the Palestinians? Lots of people live double lives, but their exploits aren't publicized. So why, then, when a preacher falls, do editors plaster it on page 1? Why do they wait for the Sunday edition — which has the largest circulation? Why jump on a noted TV evangelist who rents an expensive room at Disney World, when the publisher of the newspaper not only buys expensive condos — but keeps them full of call girls? Why single out the TV evangelist?

The answer lies in a principle outlined in James 3:1: "We who teach will be judged more strictly."

It is a matter of expectations.

The world — including the Arab world — realizes the Jews are God's chosen people. That is the reason Jews are always under the magnifying glass of the press — not because the press is anti-Semitic, but because it simply expects more of those who have been chosen by God.

The world is not threatened by godliness as much as it is hurt when those who purport godliness sometimes turn out to be just as they are. The revelation of "Why, you're no better than I am!" is a painful one to bear. The reaction is often anger.

People are longing for true heroes, but they want their heroes to be better than they are. The only way to prove they are made of genuine stuff is to try to tear them down. In short, then, don't say you are God's chosen unless you are ready to pay the price of scrutiny.

And don't complain when you are attacked, misquoted and sometimes hung out to dry in public — it's all part of the package.

Fifteen

GOOD NEWS
IS NEWS ALSO

RECENTLY ONE of America's leading journalists, George Cornell, ripped into some of his fellow editors at a gathering of the Associated Press managing editors. "Why," he asked, "do most newspapers carry an entire section of sports events daily, but only one page of religious news weekly?"

Is the news that one man bashed in the face of another man in a boxing ring really more important — or even more interesting — than the news of a young man who had an opportunity to cheat on his wife, but chose to remain faithful by relying on the power of the Holy Spirit?

That's not to say newspapers and magazines don't report on religious events. Last week when the pastor of a Pentecostal church in Indiana built a bonfire behind the church to burn rock records — and let the fire get away from him until it burned down not only the church but the local barber shop — it was reported on both NBC and CBS.

If a pastor loses his temper and goes after the bank president (who is chairman of his board) with the jawbone of an ass, then that's considered news. In fact, if he catches him at a Rotary Club meeting and clobbers him over the head in front of the district governor, it might even make the front page of the paper. Or, as recently happened, if a prominent minister is found guilty of shoplifting a copy of *Playboy* magazine from an airport newsstand, then that too makes the pages of the newspaper at some time other than in the Saturday religious page.

The press, for the most part, hangs on every word uttered by politicians and entertainers. But seldom does the press report on the words of a preacher — even if he is speaking prophetically. In other words, what comes from Washington, D.C., or Hollywood is more important than what comes from heaven.

There are exceptions, of course. The press loves to quote Billy Graham out of context when he is talking about churches behind the Iron Curtain. Reporters are notorious for editing the remarks of folks like Rex Humbard to make them sound like fools — rather than prophets. When James Robison was being attacked by homosexuals for his remarks on TV, it made every major newspaper in the nation. But when Robison publicly apologized for having been hypercritical of his Christian brothers, no one seemed to care.

And if a politician does say something with spiritual meaning, the media — including the folks who edit TV tapes — have a way of dropping that part from the published remarks.

For several years I worked for a religious magazine that edited out all references to the supernatural. Their rationale: "We'll lose credibility if we categorically state that God heals or if we mention things like speaking in tongues or miracles."

Poppycock! Americans are hungry for someone to tell them the truth about spiritual matters. Airport book racks are filled with books about the occult and demons. And newspapers know they'll lose subscribers if they don't run the horoscopes. Why, then, this conspiracy to relegate spiritual news to the religion page — and then edit it down until it reads like cold mush?

Hard-nosed editors usually look on church news as something to be tolerated. This is not just a condemnation of the news media. It is also a sad commentary on the fact that in most churches there isn't enough happening that is worth reporting.

It's when there is genuine news taking place, and that news is ignored, that I get irritated. For instance, about a month ago a young Christian housewife stopped by to visit a friend who, three times in the week before, had attempted suicide. The friend she was visiting was in deep depression. Her husband was considering having her committed to an institution to protect her and the children.

The young Christian housewife stood outside on the front walk and called on the authority of Jesus Christ. She cast out demons of depression and suicide which she felt had invaded the house and, going to her friend's bedroom, laid her hand on the woman's shoulder and prayed in tongues.

There was instant deliverance. The woman testified she felt light sweep into her mind, replacing darkness. Now the house is filled with joy. Unfortunately, that did not make the newspapers. Not even the Saturday religion page.

The news on national TV the next morning was filled with dark stories of tornadoes, nuclear threats and murders. No one seemed interested in the power of the Holy Spirit to heal a sick woman.

There is a lot of good news. If Christians would do what God told them to do — publish the glad tidings — we just might turn this wicked world right side up. Don't write me. Write your local newspaper. They just might print your story.

Sixteen

FREEDOM
TO PROBE

I SAT in the meeting room of a large hotel with a number of men and women, all leaders in the charismatic renewal.

It was one of those "ask-me-anything-you-want" meetings. I had spoken earlier in the day on the need for leaders to be transparent. Some of the men had nodded in agreement. Others responded as though I had called for glass doors on the church rest rooms.

Now we were into the question-and-answer session — throwing questions at the panel of well-known leaders. But we all knew there were certain questions no one was going to ask. It's always that way. The things we really want to know, the things we whisper about over dinner, we never ask in public — where we might get answers.

I really wanted to know, for instance, if one of the panel members had, as I had heard, prophesied that the divorce and remarriage of a certain Christian leader had been granted a special dispensation by God. I wanted to know if the divorced man's ex-wife had confirmed the prophecy.

Such prophecies, it seemed, needed to be judged by a wide spectrum of leaders — not just by the divorced man's friends or persons who were on his payroll.

It wasn't my intention to prove anything — and certainly not my intention to discredit anyone. But everyone in the room had heard the rumor, and it would have been good to get a straight answer.

However, the mere asking of the question was too embarrassing for anyone — including me — to voice it. If the rumor was false, it would sound as if we had believed the man capable of it. If it were true...?

We left the meeting still not knowing if the prophet had used God's name to bless a questionable situation.

I determined, if I was ever in a similar situation, to raise my shield against the fusillade and, jawbone swinging, attack the enemies of nuance, innuendo and rumor.

That opportunity came several months later in another leadership meeting.

A group of us were meeting in a Catholic retreat house when the subject of the marriage of Francis MacNutt came up. It was a legitimate discussion since MacNutt, who had met with us in past years, had not been invited to this session. The men — all of whom loved the former Catholic priest — were entitled to an explanation.

Some of the men in the group said they knew all the "facts" but were not free to share them with us.

All that did was intensify our curiosity.

Ever since his marriage some months before, there had been nasty rumors. It was time to put an end to them. The only way I knew to do that was by asking honest questions of those who said they knew the "facts."

I picked up my jawbone and headed for the nearest Philistine.

"Was his wife pregnant when he married her?"

What I got in return were blank stares, gulps and finally a rebuke from one of the senior members, who said the questions had reached a new low.

"We should not allow ourselves to speculate on such matters."

It was the same answer my father gave me when I was ten years old and asked him questions about my sex thoughts. "Just don't think such thoughts," he said — as though that settled everything.

My question to these responsible leaders was not a "low" question. It was designed to bring out truth.

Later in the meeting I confronted the senior member personally. He confessed that he, too, had wondered if it had been a forced marriage. But, he contended, it was none of our business.

I disagreed. I am my brother's keeper. If I am denied access to the truth about him, how can I defend him to his enemies?

Later I visited with MacNutt and his beautiful bride. I discovered that there were no secret facts. The marriage was not forced. It was a beautiful relationship and, as far as I could tell, was blessed by God.

Armed with truth, I could now defend my brother against the rumormongers. But the earlier withholding of truth had caused much damage to this man of God and his precious wife.

Facts condemn. Truth frees.

Remember, Jesus did not say, "Ye shall know the *facts*, and they shall make you free."

That's one of the differences between the secular and the Christian media. A magazine like *Charisma & Christian Life* is commissioned to print not just facts — but truth.

On some occasions facts would cause harm if published, so they are omitted. But to refuse to write about an event simply because it is painful — or even offensive to some — binds rather than makes us free.

Occasionally in our editorial meetings the question arises: Should this magazine print that story? There are certain criteria which should always be applied:

- Do we have all the facts, and can they be substantiated?
- Do we know the truth behind the facts?
- By publishing the story, which may reflect negatively upon some individual or institution, do we bring greater glory to God and His kingdom?
- Will the story strengthen the body of Christ, or does it merely satisfy morbid curiosity?
- Are we willing to brave the onslaught of people who are threatened by truth — even lose some subscriptions — in order to warn, point out dangerous trends or bring a corrective word?
- Are we willing to kill a story, even though it is factual, if we are convinced it will do more harm than good by publishing it?

The secular media believe, for the most part, that the only reason for not publishing a story would be the threat to national security. (Yet the publication of instructions on how to make an atomic bomb in your garage makes one wonder if even that re-striction has now been lifted.)

The Christian media operate on different — higher — stand-ards. They operate on the basis of truth, not fact.

The Bible is our guide. Here we find the story of David's adul-terous affair with Bathsheba, but the story is told redemptively. Millions have been helped by reading it.

I am grateful for a free press. It has its origins in the Judeo-Christian faith. We do not have to look beyond Watergate to see how a free press helped save our nation.

But the Christian media have an even greater responsibility to go beyond facts to truth — always for the purpose of redemption and edification.

Some people always will be offended by truth. I am offended by rumors. That's the reason honest questions between brothers and sisters are never out of order in the kingdom of God.

Part Four

———

ON THE POWER
THAT RUNS
THE KINGDOM

Seventeen

THE REAL POWER
RUNS DEEP

S EVERAL YEARS ago my family and I spent some time with our friends Larry and Devi Titus in Washington state. One afternoon Larry took me through one of those big dams on the Columbia River where so much of the electric power for the Northwest is produced.

I had heard of such things as turbines, power plants and generators. But for some reason I had always thought the power from those big dams was provided by the water which rolled over the spillway. It never occurred to me — a flatlander from Florida — that the real power was not in the froth which splattered over the top of the dam but was produced in the hidden machines far below the surface.

We took an elevator deep into the mysterious innards of the dam. Stepping out into a huge room — as long as the dam was wide — I was suddenly in the middle of more power than I had ever dreamed possible. It wasn't noisy or spectacular. In fact, the room was almost empty except for the huge cranes overhead on their tracks. The power seemed to be contained in a deep "hummm" that literally vibrated into the marrow of my bones.

I could almost imagine myself stepping into that room mentioned in Acts 4 where all the believers were in deep prayer. The

Bible says the building itself actually vibrated as they prayed.

Deep in the floor of the dam, with only the tips of the spindles showing, were the mighty turbines. That afternoon only five of the nine turbines were in operation. But that was enough to provide power for half the state of Washington and part of Oregon.

We stayed for a long time, walking slowly, almost reverently, the length of the room — feeling the sound of those mighty turbines turning ever so slowly beneath our feet.

Hundreds of feet above us, and for many miles behind us, the huge lake pushed against the propellers of the machines. The pressure of that water — millions of pounds of pressure — turned the turbines to generate hundreds of thousands of kilowatt hours of electricity.

We took the elevator back to the top of the dam. Walking out on the catwalk, we watched the water from the spillway splash in a spectacular waterfall. It, too, was part of the process. When the pressure on the dam became too great, caused by high water in the lake, the spillways would be opened. If the water in the lake was low, there was no waterfall over the dam.

But it was those silent, hidden turbines which produced the power — even though there was no outer display of their might.

It is so easy to get enchanted by the spectacular — the outer manifestations. Occasionally we will have visitors stop by our church on a Sunday. If that happens to be a service in which there are no spectacular gifts in operation — no tongues, no prophecy, no healings — they sometimes leave disappointed. They thought the power of the Holy Spirit was in the outward signs.

I thank God for continued Pentecost: tongues, prophecies, healings and miracles. These were normal in the New Testament church; they should be present in the church of today.

But I am convinced we must never confuse spillway Christianity with the power of the Holy Spirit.

The water over the dam plays a vital purpose. It is something of a release for the rising tide of spirituality. In fact, if the lake is low, there will be no outward signs. If the lake is high, you can expect an overflow whenever the body gets together.

The reason there has been such a mighty display of the gifts of the Spirit over the last several years has to do with the latter rain which has been falling in the mountains.

Now even denominational lakes are filling up — and spillways are merrily splashing all over the place.

I pray our lakes will remain high. I love it when I meet with a group of people who are "prayed up," "paid up" and "praised up." Folks like this are going to overflow. There's no way to stop them — unless you want to run the risk of a broken dam.

But I hope we will never equate the power of the Holy Spirit with outward signs. Regardless of whether a church displays the spectacular (and they will if the water is high), the Holy Spirit is still turning the turbines. Unless, that is, the lake has gone dry.

However, it is possible for a church — or an individual Christian — never to have any display of the spectacular and still be used by God to accomplish great things.

In other words, it is possible to have your water level far below the spillway crest and yet have your turbines still turn. Some of my finest sermons were preached when my lake was at its lowest level. In fact, there have been times when I have felt completely drained, only to find when I laid my hand on some sick person he was instantly healed.

The absence of outward signs does not mean God is not generating power through your life. It simply means your lake is probably low. The power that runs the kingdom is not limited to the overflow. Indeed, most of that is not power at all but merely evidence of a high level of enthusiasm. It is possible to have a huge spillway display and produce no power whatsoever — because your turbines are clogged with debris. The power that runs the kingdom is found in the dynamos of men's hearts as they love one another, as they serve one another, as they give to one another, as they pray for one another.

Granted, God says He loves our praise. He loves our enthusiasm. He loves it when we clap our hands and shout for joy. He goes so far as to say He abides in the praises of His people.

But it is possible to heal the sick, deliver the possessed, even raise the dead and still be outside the will of God.

God does not judge us on the basis of charisma — but on the basis of character. Do we keep our word? Do we hold grudges? Are we generous? Are we loyal to each other? Are we full of love for our heavenly Father? And for His children?

I thank God for spillway Christians — those who make a big splash. But those who provide the real power are often hidden, seldom noticed. On such does the kingdom of God depend.

Eighteen

MOVIN' IN A
SLOW HURRY

I GREW up under the tutorage of a wonderful old Southern "black mammy" named Willie Mae McGriff. She was an intimate part of our family for more than thirty years. It was she who taught me the art of being in what she called a "slow hurry."

There were mornings when she arrived at our house moving slow. My mother, who was hyper and sometimes demanding, would push her a little. I remember Willie Mae's delightful response: "Don't worry 'bout that, Miz B. I'll get it done. Today I's just movin' in a *slow hurry*."

What a great way to accomplish the important things!

It was this lesson King David learned so painfully when it came time to return the ark of the covenant after it had been released from captivity by the Philistines. Eager to have the ark placed in its new home atop Mt. Zion, David commandeered the first vehicle he could find. It turned out to be an ox cart pulled by a couple of milk cows. That didn't matter to David as long as he got the job done.

While God is a God of enthusiasm (the word *enthusiasm*, you may know, comes from two Greek words, *en theos*, meaning "in God"), man's problem is confusing genuine spiritual excitement with impetuousness. Too many of us act like old steam locomotives — blowing off all the power in the whistle and saving little to turn the wheels.

David was not interested in means. His job as commander was to secure the ark on Mt. Zion — as quickly as possible. Away they went, singing and dancing in the victory.

The story of what happened when David got ahead of God — and tried to do God's work using man's method — is classic. Depending on organization rather than charisma, he assigned men to hurry the process. To David the completion of the task was far more important than the method used. The results were tragic. When the ark tilted on the cart and one of the men reached up to steady it, he was struck dead. That's heavy stuff. It was God's way of saying He is more interested in the way a thing is done than whether it is completed.

After losing one of his top men because of his haste, David slowed down. He left the ark at the house of a fellow named Obed-Edom. He returned to Jerusalem to do a little Bible study. When all else fails, read the instruction manual.

Three months later he returned for the ark. But his attitude had changed, as well as his methods. No longer was he impetuous. This time he was willing to move in a *slow hurry*.

How had he changed?

He had *studied* the Bible.

He had *sought counsel* from wise men.

He was determined to *follow God's plan* — no matter how foolish it seemed.

He *communicated* with his people.

He *organized* his men.

Finally, he *moved ahead*, but only six steps at a time. After each stage he stopped the procession. They took time to build an altar, offer sacrifices and celebrate before moving on another six steps and repeating the entire process. He was moving in a *slow hurry* — right on God's time schedule.

I shudder when I consider all the projects going on in the kingdom. God has a perfect way for His people to evangelize the world, to spread the gospel through the media, to raise money for building projects. Yet every place I go, following the ark up the road, I hear the sounds of the ox cart.

I wonder: Could it be that God is more interested in how we raise money than the amount we raise?

My old jungle pilot friend, Bob Griffin, reminds me that those early World War I fighter planes had no slow speeds. When Eddie Rickenbacker and the Red Baron were dueling over France, their aircraft engines had two power positions: full on and full off.

The fact is, those early rotary engines didn't have an adjustable throttle. That was a later invention. All they had was an off/on switch.

At "contact" the engine bellowed into an immediate full-throated roar. Woe to the pilot who wasn't pointed in the right direction when some luckless private hand-propped the engine. From that moment on, the engine was running at full rpms.

Getting the plane back on the ground was even more exciting than taking off. It was done by killing the engine through "blipping" the ignition with a switch on the joystick — alternately shutting the power off and letting it come back on, a series of loud roars each followed by deadly silence.

Pilots of today's planes know the danger of running at full throttle. While it is necessary to get off the ground and clear obstructions, full power will quickly burn out an engine. That probably applies to the number of meetings a person can attend in a week as well.

Paul Garlington, a pastor in Rochester, New York, says folks sometimes ask what he is doing on a certain day. When he says, "Nothing," they try to move in. "You don't understand," Paul tells them. "I'm occupied that day. I'm doing Nothing."

I know a lot of people who have only two speeds — full power and off. They keep passing me in life at full speed. I envy them for their ability to get a lot done in a short period. Yet as I plod down the road like the proverbial tortoise racing the hare, I often see their burned-out ruins.

No engine, especially the human engine, is designed to run at full power.

Throttle back occasionally. Stop and study. Happiness and health come when you learn to move in a *slow hurry*.

Believe it or not, God is not depending on you — He wants you to depend on Him.

Nineteen

LEARNING
TO LEAN

I WAS a senior in college before I committed my life to Jesus Christ. But it wasn't a full commitment. Even though I intended to trust God, I felt I needed to trust my own understanding also — and my ability to work things out. After all, I had never trusted anyone completely, and this was a big step.

What I did was share my trust with God. In short, I planned to do my best and let God take care of the deficiencies. That kind of partial trust was not based on a lack of desire to trust, only a lack of ability.

One has to *learn* to trust God. Just as we've learned to distrust human nature because we've been disappointed by people who have let us down, just as we've learned the hard way that no piece of equipment is fully trustworthy, so we have to learn to trust God.

Much of the problem lies in what we have to unlearn. Since I have learned to distrust people, since I know my car battery or alternator could betray me at any moment, since I know through experience that the airlines are often late — I am not willing to trust God fully.

Perhaps, I think, God can handle the big things such as the end of the world or the ultimate outcome of good over evil. But when it comes to trusting Him with relatively minor things — like providing me with enough money to live on — well, I'm not so sure.

I have to learn He can be trusted by trusting.

For over forty years Eunice Pike has worked with the Mazatec Indians in southwestern Mexico.

The Mazatec people seldom wish anyone well. Not only that, they are hesitant to teach another or to share the gospel with each other.

Eunice says this odd behavior stems from the Indians' concept of "limited good." They believe there is only so much good, so much knowledge, so much love to go around. To teach another means you might drain yourself of knowledge. To love a second child means you have to love the first child less. To wish someone well — "Have a good day" — means you have just given away some of your own happiness, which cannot be re-acquired because there is only so much to go around.

A lot of Christians seem to think this way too. They trust God, but deep inside they suspect God is not an unlimited resource. True, they believe God owns the cattle on a thousand hills, but they suspect his herd may be running thin. After all, a lot of people are eating beef these days. Therefore, they lean on their own understanding and pen up a few cattle in their backyard — just in case they go to God's meat market one day and find the cupboard bare, or the truckers have gone on strike and aren't delivering anymore.

I battle with this constantly when it comes to money. Since God is like my father, I was taught, then there is always a possibility I may go to Him one day with a request for funds (as I often did to my dad) only to be told there are other needs more pressing. "You'll have to wait until some rich South African gives his tithes, because God's coffers have run dry," the stone-faced angel with the green bookkeeper's visor will say.

Believing, therefore, that God is a limited resource, I am guarded on how much I give. I want to give more, but if I give God's money away, there is a chance it will never be replaced.

I remember Pat Robertson interviewing a wealthy celebrity following the celebrity's conversion to Christianity. The man alluded to this same concept, saying he gave everything to God — but he did hold back about $200,000 in case of a rainy day.

Pat's comment was that the man must have been expecting a

second deluge.

We want to trust but have been taught that God is like man — stingy, disinterested, self-centered and surely limiting on His resources.

It's best summed up in the slogan that came out of World War II: "God is my co-pilot." In other words, I'm captain of this ship. It is under my control. God is welcome aboard. In fact, I'm delighted for Him to sit in the co-pilot's seat in case there is an emergency. But I'll not call on Him until I need Him, and even then I want Him to remember I'm still in command.

We apply the same concept in our ministries. We have church committee meetings and mission board meetings, or we plan grand schemes to win the world. We analyze, consider from every angle, use the counsel of men and make judgments which we feel sure are God's will or program. But we are really trusting ourselves. We trust our ability to take a certain business (or scriptural) formula and apply it to the kingdom of God to raise money, to recruit volunteers, to build a mailing list, to increase attendance, to ensure monthly donations. "Do it this way, and it will work every time," we're told.

But the question still haunts me: What if we took all our abilities and laid them humbly on the altar and trusted God?

It's worth a try. And how else will we learn to lean?

Twenty

THE SPIRIT OF
THE WORLD

THE HEAD of a large missionary organization told me it was being sued by two of its members. These people had earlier dedicated their lives to missions. Now they have various ailments. One man has ulcers. A woman who lived in the tropics has skin cancer. A "Christian" lawyer, hearing of their problems, advised them to sue the missionary organization. Their afflictions, he said, were "job related."

The mission director shook his head. "They were willing to give their lives — but I guess that didn't include stomach and skin."

The missionaries and their lawyer have been infected with what Paul called "the spirit of the world" (1 Cor. 2:12).

Despite the classic Pentecostal definition, worldliness (the Greek word is *kosmos*) is far more than cosmetics. It is also more than R-rated movies or X-rated prostitutes.

Worldliness is focusing on the things of time rather than things eternal.

The sin of today's Pentecostal leaders is not sexual impropriety — acts hardly worth mentioning. The real problem is a life stance which focuses on the visible earthly kingdom rather than the invisible kingdom of God. It's evidenced by incomprehensible

71

wealth, overwhelming debt, ungodly fund raising and lavish homes.

It's sad that the muted lips of the Assemblies of God were only able to blow the whistle *after* their former heroes were caught. Sad, because worldliness is far more than smoking and sex. Sad, because many Assemblies of God leaders were emulating the same materialism exhibited by those now trapped in their own webs, paralyzing the denomination's power to police except when it came to outward acts.

Americans — most of whom are middle class and caught in their own worldliness — see us taking offerings from the poor in order to feather our beds. They call us Cadillac Christians and wonder why we don't give away more than we keep. They seem to know God has called us to walk by a different standard and are angry when we don't.

Too many of our leaders resemble the worldly sons of Eli — Hophni and Phinehas — who "treated the Lord's offering with contempt." These forerunners of today's prosperity preachers enjoyed temple living, eating the fat which should have been used as a burnt sacrifice. Because of them God put the death curse of Ichabod on the entire nation.

The spirit of the world has infected all of us. We see it in the struggling black churches where the poor, unable to rise from their poverty, elevate their pastors to the role of king.

We see it in the once-poor Pentecostal churches which, having ridden the charismatic wave across the tracks, now rival the downtown banks and hotels in plush materialism.

We see it in the liturgical churches which have gold-plated the cross as a status symbol. Their clergymen, who are sometimes imitated by uptown Pentecostals, dress themselves in royal robes, title themselves "reverends" and drive royal chariots for one reason: status.

Tell me, can you picture Jesus dressed in scarlet and wearing a dangling cross?

And what about the rest of us? We spend millions on self while giving pennies to missions. Our American brand of Christianity has become a wealthy counterculture which no longer cares about the image it projects. For every soul won to Christ by our flashy buildings and multimillion-dollar television ministries, there are millions who drive by, angry at the injustice these money-suckers represent. We brag about being New Testament Christians while living the life-style of Nero.

We have become like Demas, who deserted Paul "because he loved this world" (2 Tim. 4:10).

I recall the opening statement made by Francis MacNutt at the Holy Spirit Conference in Jerusalem in 1976: "If Jesus were on earth, He wouldn't be here today. He couldn't afford the registration."

We have forgotten who Jesus was — and how He lived.

As a kid I thought the ushers took the offering up into the belfry and burned it as a sacrifice. That was before I knew about preachers who used it to buy gold faucets.

"The greatest task with which the church is confronted," Dietrich Bonhoeffer reportedly said from his Nazi prison, "is to teach people how to live in this world." And, I add, without letting the world live in us.

So we have two problems: what to do with the bodies of our fallen comrades and how to keep from falling ourselves.

Commenting on this, Roy Hicks Jr. said he was reminded of David's attitude toward the death of Saul. He lamented his fall and sent his mighty men to rescue the bodies of Saul and Jonathan. "While we must not compromise the standards of righteousness for leaders," Hicks says, "we also must not allow the 'bodies' of those who have fallen to remain exposed for the devouring analysis of a fallen world."

The confused folks of this culture — who judge us by the behavior of a few — are looking for a breed of people who are different, who are not in bondage to the world as they are. The only way we will ever restore our lost credibility is to pick up our wounded, renounce what we have become and recommit to be like Jesus.

73

Twenty-one

WORSHIPPING
MAN IS WRONG

RUSSELL DILDAY, president of Southwestern Baptist Theological Seminary in Fort Worth, Texas, the world's largest seminary, told of an interview with Billy Graham. Graham was asked who would be the leaders of the evangelical world in the future. He answered: "The next leaders of the evangelical world will not be individuals but institutions."

If that's true, it's frightening. Institutions breed death because they are impersonal. Man-worship — whether it's worshipping Kenneth Copeland or even your local pastor — is wrong. But worshipping an institution is worse. Men usually don't declare themselves "great" or "incomparable" — but institutions do. And the moment they do they sign their own spiritual death warrant.

Church historians mark the downfall of institutions to when they begin composing hymns to themselves — as the Salvation Army did some years ago. We find that same syndrome in many large churches whose press releases describe them as "the best," "the biggest" or "the friendliest." A signboard along the highway proclaims: "The great Calvary Cathedral will meet all your spiritual needs." Sad. We've come a long way from singing, "God will take care of you."

As a college student I always felt uncomfortable singing the alma mater. I could never choke out those final lines:

> Hail to thee, O alma mater,
> Mercer, hail, all hail.

Now I know why. The Spirit living in me would not allow me to venerate any institution any more than I can pay homage to a man. Both Nero and Caligula understood this as the line of spiritual demarcation with those early Christians. Rather than sing the Roman alma mater they lined up by the thousands to say, *"Christus este kurios,"* and went bravely to the crosses and lions.

Is it wrong, as the Jehovah's Witnesses say, to salute the flag? No. It is right to "pledge allegiance" — just as it is right to take vows to marriage, to military service, to your job or to a local church. But to pay homage — to say "All hail!" — to man or institution borders on, and indeed may be, idolatry.

The problem with institutions is, left unchecked, they soon evolve into personification, taking on themselves the characteristics of men yet remaining impersonal.

The common man is looking for security. If he can find it in a doctrine, he cherishes that doctrine. If he finds it in a man, he idolizes the man. If he finds it in an institution, he quickly becomes a piece of machinery fitted into a system which by its nature is forced to clip and trim the sprouting gifts of the Spirit until all the plants look the same.

Take away a man's security and he panics. But if his security is in Jesus, he is not affected by growing doctrine, falling men or iron-clad institutions.

Institutions demand constant feeding — supplying oil to the gears of the machinery. Take "storehouse tithing," which is a prime Old Testament principle. This doctrine insinuates that only the clergy are smart enough and spiritual enough to distribute kingdom funds. Why, then, do I give my tithe through my local church? Not out of biblical command, for I believe the New Testament teaches each man should seek the Lord's best as to where it should be placed. Rather, I tithe through my local church because I believe I should give my tithe where I am fed spiritually.

Offerings over and above my tithe are given to various ministries as the Lord directs.

If, for some unthinkable reason, I were part of a church which was not feeding me spiritually, if I belonged to a church which wasted money on unneeded luxuries, if my church sent part of my money to humanistic and communistic councils — then I would not give my money to that church. The same is true of sending offerings to parachurch ministries — evangelistic, missionary or television — which use that money unwisely on worldly things. That would be poor stewardship.

Institutional thinking, however, does not allow that kind of freedom. It demands the tithe for it does not want its constituency to think independently — or even think at all. The institution realizes that where your treasure is, there is your heart as well — so it demands your money.

People need to be taught to give to God, not to institutions.

Graham may be right when he says the shift is toward institutions. That's part of the cycle which begins with charismatic personalities and evolves into the institutions they create. Oral Roberts, Pat Robertson, Kenneth Hagin, Bill Bright — all are building institutions of higher learning. I'm seeing it in my own church, which has now grown large and is becoming structured. The next step is institutionalization.

Is that wrong? No, it is inevitable. It becomes wrong only if the leadership becomes institutionalized in its thinking and refuses to allow the people to hear for themselves.

But it's sad. I fear that sometime over the next thirty years a group of people will do as we did half a generation ago — pull out (or be kicked out) and start a "New Testament church." Not that our church has drifted from the New Testament forms. In fact, we are closer in structure now than we were when we started. But what of the Spirit?

Jesus' church was a band of people in relationship — to Him and to each other. They did not honor the group. They did not speak of the great Church of the Disciples. But under Constantine the church institutionalized — and the battle has been going on ever since.

So what do we do? The best we can — and fight to remain free.

I don't want to be numbered among those who were left behind when the cloud moved because I refused to submit to an earthly Moses who was anointed by God. But if I align myself too closely, I may die with him on Nebo. I must remember: Canaan, not Moses, is my final goal.

Twenty-two

USING
THE NAME

I ARRIVED at the new Founders' Inn on the Christian Broadcasting Network campus on a Thursday afternoon. I was to be Pat Robertson's guest on "The 700 Club" Friday morning, then speak that night at the CBN partners' banquet in the hotel ballroom.

The magnificent hotel had been open only five weeks. They were still laying sod. I was impressed with the hotel staff. The bell captain, I discovered, was a graduate of both Oral Roberts University and Asbury Seminary. He had been a Methodist pastor before assuming his new position. (He indicated this was a step up in his career.)

The hotel was crowded that weekend because of the partners' seminar. Every room was taken. After checking in, I picked up my bag, walked around the lake past the physical fitness building and on to the James River Lodge.

When I unlocked the door, however, I was in for a surprise. The room didn't have a bed. Just a sofa, some chairs and a couple of tables.

Strange. I began opening doors. Closet. Bathroom. No bed. A double door led to another room, but it was locked. I walked out in the hall and asked one of the housekeepers if she would come

77

look.

"It's our best room," she smiled. "We reserve it especially for visiting speakers."

"Ah...it doesn't have a bed."

"Don't worry," she said. "We'll come in later this evening and fold down the sofa."

Maybe none of the rooms in this new hotel has beds, I thought. I walked down the hall and peeked in a couple of rooms. They all had beds. I seemed to be the only one in the hotel who was going to have to sleep on the sofa. Maybe the others had beds because they were large contributors. I blushed when I thought of the meager amount I had sent CBN last year. "You get what you give," I'd preached. I'd just take what was mine and try to be thankful.

That night, trying to get comfortable on my four-inch-thick mattress that rested on an iron bar that went across the middle of my back, I thought I heard God say, "Sleeping on the sofa is good for you."

"It's not very good for my back," I replied.

"No, it's good for your soul. People who think they are important need to sleep on sofas every once in a while. Just be thankful you're not sleeping on the ground."

The next morning, following my television appearance, Jackie Mitchum-Yocky, the guest coordinator, asked how I slept.

"There wasn't a bed in my room. I had to sleep on a sofa."

She was aghast.

"I heard it was a miracle hotel," I said. "But when I stood in the middle of the room and confessed 'Bed!' — nothing happened. I figured my faith wasn't strong enough."

Jackie got action, however. That afternoon when I returned to my room, the door to the adjoining room had been opened. There, just a door away, was a beautiful king-sized bed. The sheets were all folded down, and little candies lay on the pillow. It had waited for me all night, only I couldn't get to it. I didn't have a room — I had a suite.

It wasn't a wipeout, however. I told the story that night at the partners' banquet — encouraging them to keep giving to CBN if they expected a bed the next time they visited. Afterward, my old friend Scott Ross said it was my fault. All I had to do, he said, was "invoke the name" and I would have had a bed.

"Around here, there's one name that opens every door," he said. "Just say, 'I'm Pat Robertson's guest,' and you get action."

Back home I told the story again — this time to my grandchildren. Eight-year-old Dusty reminded me I should have done what David did when he went into battle against Goliath. "You come against me with a sword and spear and javelin," he told the giant, "but I come against you in the *name of the Lord Almighty*."

That's powerful stuff. Even more powerful is what Jesus told His followers:

"Whatever you ask in My name, that I will do" (John 14:13, NKJV).

Praying in the name of Jesus is more than tacking a formula to the end of a prayer. It is praying in full harmony with God's wishes and values. It is agreeing with the nature and essence of God. It is calling on His entire administration. When God announced His mighty presence in Psalm 75:1 (KJV), it was said, "Thy name is near."

I'll remember that the next time I don't have a bed — or when another giant appears, trying to kill me.

Twenty-three

THE CHALLENGE
OF EXCELLENCE

PSYCHOLOGIST CARL Rogers once said, "The older I grow the more I understand those things most private to us are also those things most universal."

Inside each of us is a little person, stretching, striving, looking at the impossible and saying, I can do that.

Last week I reread Margaret Craven's novel *I Heard the Owl Call My Name*. It's a haunting story of a young, dying priest who finds the meaning of life when he is sent by his wise bishop to minister to a tribe of vanishing Indians in the Pacific Northwest. When I finished, I lay back on my bed, closed my eyes and said, "I can write like that. I know I can."

It was the beauty of the writing — as much as the message — which captivated me. This deep admiration for craftsmanship stirs up all the slumbering gifts in me, priming my soul to achieve.

As a boy I used to attend the street dances in the mountains of Western North Carolina. Watching the flashing feet, swirling skirts and taps rat-a-tatting in the pavement as the mountain cloggers kicked their heels to bluegrass music, I knew I could do it too. But my feet were chained by a legalistic theology. All I was allowed to do was stand on the curb and watch as the dancers did "the single shuffle," "the earl" and "the chicken." Now the chains are off. Last week I purchased a bluegrass music record featuring "The Battle of New Orleans." A local cobbler has added jingle taps to an old pair of shoes, and I've ordered a book called *Mountain Clogging — You Can Do It*. Just you wait. It's time to dance.

It's been inside me all along, that drive to create with excellence. It's part of the image of the Creator Himself.

I doubt if Oliver Wendell Holmes had clogging in mind when he challenged himself to "build thee more stately mansions, O my soul." But the theme is the same. Some build their stately mansions in the science lab, others in the kitchen, some in the animal breeding pens and some at the keyboard. But regardless of how it manifests itself, the drive is spiritual. You look at a model and say, "I can do that too." To do less is the greatest of all tragedies.

Thomas Gray, lamenting over the tombstones in a country churchyard, reflected on the sadness of wasted excellence and wrote:

> Perhaps in this neglected spot is laid
> Some heart once pregnant with celestial fire:
> Hands, that the rod of empire might have swayed.
> Or wak'd to ecstasy the living lyre.

The models of excellence are those that wake me to ecstasy. When I listen to my old Fritz Krysler records and hear the master violinist playing "Barcarole" and "The Rosary"; when I sit in a jungle village and watch a trained linguist conversing with a dark-skinned tribesman in a never-before-written language; when I watch a helicopter pilot thread his airship between towering trees and steep boulders; when I watch my artist-daughter take charcoal and paper and create beauty out of nothing — my eyes grow moist. I, too, my heart says, can achieve.

These are the stimulators of my life — the ones who prime my pump. Thank you, Whittier, Whitman and Longfellow. Thank you, Shakespeare, Kipling and Tennyson. Even today, long years after I was forced to read you in English Lit 102, I take your books from my shelves to read aloud to no one but myself.

Thank you, all the men and women I have never met who have enriched my life with your excellence and challenged me to the finer things by daring to achieve.

Last year I put on a surgical gown and accompanied one of the world's leading ophthalmologists into the operating theatre. For two hours I stood beside Dr. Jim Gills as he removed cataracts and implanted lenses in the eyes of a dozen patients. Watching his skilled fingers through the microscope, I felt something welling up inside me. It was the same feeling an expectant mother must have when she feels life moving in her body — "pregnant with celestial fire." I almost exploded from the operating room into the waiting room, where my wife was sitting with my mother who was scheduled as the next patient. Tearing off my face mask I blurted, "I can do that too if I have a chance."

My mother's face blanched white. "Not on me, you won't," she said defiantly, and she rose to walk out.

Of course, I didn't — on her or anyone else. It takes years of discipline to reach that place. But seeing a master surgeon at work stimulated the creative part of me — the God part — which says, Nothing is impossible. Don't ever give up.

Every place I turn I find those who are doing things better than I will ever do them. But I am not discouraged by their excellence; instead, I am challenged and motivated. Jesus threw down the gauntlet when He dared us to achieve spiritual perfection — "even as your Father which is in heaven is perfect" (see Matt. 5:48, KJV). Impossible? Absolutely not. God blesses the one who strives to achieve, for he's a winner, regardless of how well anyone else does. The standard can be reached by all because our model, Jesus Himself, "controls and urges and impels us" onward (2 Cor. 5:14, AMP).

I am grateful for all the models, the heroes, the winners — those who excel and achieve. In them, as in Jesus, I see the reflection of the Creator. Because of them I am inspired onward — toward excellence.

Twenty-four

CHISELED IN CRUMBLING CONCRETE

THE IDEA of taking spiritual inventory for the purpose of considering what part of our religious life needs to be changed — or discarded — is distasteful to most Christians. And heretical to others. We like to believe there are some things so sacred they should never be touched, questioned or changed.

As a believer, however, I must constantly question, examine and re-evaluate my doctrine. To do otherwise will style me as a dried wineskin. I will then be forced to reject anything new or different for fear it will cause me to change my life-style.

Actually, I believe very little of what I believed twenty years ago. Oh, I still believe in the essentials — the divinity of Christ, the sovereignty of God, the inspiration of the Bible, the virgin birth and so on. Yet even my concepts of these have changed across the years.

I remember the time some years ago, as our family was emerging from its Baptist cocoon, that we ventured to serve communion at our dinner table. I asked my daughter Robin, then about fourteen, to pray before we took the elements. Her little prayer was devastating.

"Thank You, Jesus, for Your blood we're about to drink."

I tried not to show my dismay as I corrected her. "Honey, that's a sweet prayer, but we're not drinking Jesus' blood. This juice is merely a symbol of His blood."

"But, Daddy," she said innocently, "that's not what the Bible says. Jesus says, 'This is My blood.' "

As a Bible-believer I was trapped in my own web. This incident was the beginning of a period of spiritual growth which moved me from symbolist to sacramentalist. I find myself now standing with the Lutherans, proclaiming the "real presence" of Jesus in the elements. And who knows where I'll go from here?

Yesterday, sorting through some papers in the bottom drawer of my desk, I discovered an old article I had clipped from *Reader's Digest* eleven years ago. The print was fading, and it was yellowed around the edges. The author was the renowned international architect Peter Blake. Why, I wondered, had I clipped this particular article all those years ago and dropped it into my desk drawer? I picked it up and read the first paragraph.

"There exists a great temptation, in the life of an artist or scientist or modern architect like myself, to commit oneself to a dogma in one's youth and then to build one's entire work on that foundation. Unhappily for me and some of my friends, the premises upon which we have almost literally built our world are crumbling."

Then I remembered why I had clipped the article. Blake was not talking about just architecture. He was talking about life. My life. He was talking about my relationship with God. I read on.

"We have begun to discover that almost nothing that we were taught by our betters in or out of the architecture schools of the mid-century has stood the test of time. Nothing — or almost nothing — turns out to have been entirely true" (*Reader's Digest*, May 1975, p. 163).

I let my mind drift back to that opening day on the campus of Southwestern Baptist Theological Seminary in Ft. Worth, Texas. Fresh from college with a degree in English literature, I was eager to get started on my theological training.

Wandering about the campus, I discovered, chiseled on the cornerstone of the library, a portion of Scripture which was the heraldic insignia of the seminary: "As ye go, preach..." (Matt. 10:7).

The verse, however, like everything I had been taught, was incomplete. Preach what? Where there should have been a practical application there was only an ellipsis — three dots signifying there was more, but that it wasn't important.

The founding fathers of that great theological seminary (and I still believe it is the finest in the world) were walking as best they could in the light they had. Their mistake came, perhaps, when they determined to chisel their theology — with all its incompleteness — in stone. As a result, a lot of us in that mid-century generation did as Peter Blake did: We committed ourselves to a dogma in our youth which later turned out to be not entirely true.

I am not angry at my theological forefathers, just a bit sad. No one ever explained the rest of that verse. "As ye go, preach, saying, The kingdom of heaven is at hand. Heal the sick, cleanse the lepers, raise the dead, cast out devils: freely ye have received, freely give" (Matt. 10:7-8, KJV).

Instead of explaining, they explained it away.

Unquestioned dogmas and creeds are poison to life in Christ. A well-known and much-respected Pentecostal teacher once stated, with more seriousness than his audience appreciated, "The old-time Pentecostals saw miracles, while this new breed just talks about them. In fact, as long as they were illiterate they were filled with supernatural power. Then they learned to write, and the first thing they wrote was a creed. In so doing they quenched the Holy Spirit."

I am not defending ignorance. Nor illiteracy. I am simply pointing out that creeds, like those tiny shoes worn by Japanese women, deform and sometimes kill. Growth and accompanying change must be part of our walk with Christ.

Kathryn Kuhlman once told me, "I've found something that works, and I'll never change."

But she did change. She died.

Is there nothing unchangeable? Oh, yes! God! But to become like Him means even our sacred things must be laid on the altar. For I suspect that when we get to heaven we'll discover our doctrine was, after all, quite different from God's doctrine.

Twenty-five

WHO DEFINES
"CORRECT DOCTRINE"?

COTTON MATHER, the seventeenth-century Puritan leader in New England, told the story of the bees.

Bees, Mather discovered, swarm in tribes. However, the tribes are constantly battling each other because they smell differently. Only when the bees are covered with the correct pollen and nectar do they work together peacefully.

Mather, in typical Puritan fashion, assigned "correct doctrine" as the pollen. He felt Christians — especially tribal Christians — would always fight with each other until they were covered with pure doctrine.

Pure doctrine is important. But who among us is qualified to define it? As I look around I find that no one, not even my wife, totally agrees with my doctrine. In fact, I don't even agree with myself, for I keep changing as I grow older and receive more revelation (or is it illumination?).

If you examine the New Testament you do not find Jesus urging His followers to check each other's doctrine — much as a mechanic might check the oil in your automobile.

In fact, the concept of a doctrinal dipstick is totally foreign to the Spirit of Jesus, who taught instead about specks and beams.

A friend of mine is an airplane mechanic. Every day he goes

into his shop and picks up what is known in the trade as a "squawk sheet." With it he ticks off all the things wrong with the airplane engine he is working on.

A squawk sheet has its purpose. It's good to discover what is wrong with an airplane engine — especially when it is on the ground. Metal filings in the oil filter indicate the engine just might stop running some day. That's unfortunate if you're in the clouds at nine thousand feet over the Great Gooey Tarpits of Idaho.

And a loose gasket on the fuel line is a real danger signal. Unless it is tightened, your plane just might burst into flames.

Thus the squawk sheet serves a real purpose.

But serious problems arise if my friend, the mechanic, tries to carry this same mentality into the church business meeting. Or when a group of pastors get together to talk about what's wrong with national ministries.

Does this mean we should shut our eyes to the metal filings in the ORU or "700 Club" oil filter? That we should wink at the loose gasket in some TV ministry or ignore the fact that the Roman Catholic church badly needs an oil change? Not so.

The question is: Are we called to be spiritual mechanics?

Honestly, friends, I'm having a hard enough time getting my own doctrine straightened out. I need help, but only when it is offered in love without threat of rejection.

I like what David said: "Let the godly smite me! It will be a kindness! If they reprove me, it is medicine! Don't let me refuse it" (Ps. 141:5, TLB).

But there is a vast difference between a dose of medicine from a godly friend and waking in the middle of the night and finding your room full of doctrinal detectives looking under your bed.

As a friend says, "I used to have wings, but that was before the backbiters chewed them off."

Several years ago it was chic for charismatics to sneer at Ft. Lauderdale, headquarters of Christian Growth Ministries. Our squawk sheet was filled with items like "deliverance," "discipleship" and so forth.

Then it was the Tulsa Boys who became the target for our criticism. Those of us who have never seen a vision at all criticized Oral Roberts, who said he saw a vision of Jesus putting His arms around the City of Faith.

And from our sickbeds we sneer at Kenneth Hagin because he hasn't been sick in forty-seven years.

And we say, "Hmm, looks like metal filings in the Tulsa oil filter. Better keep that overseas plane on the ground and put the passengers on a rusty old tramp steamer leaving next year."

Sure there are extremes. A story was going around California that an entire church died from an overdose of faith confession.

But the problem is that while I'm out nipping (I don't really backbite; I just nip) at others, my own church is about to fall to pieces around me.

When was the last time you heard anyone give unreserved praise to anything? "Yes, but" has almost replaced "Praise the Lord" on the lips of many charismatics.

I was in a leaders' meeting one time with T. L. Osborn of Tulsa. Osborn has spent much of his life preaching in underdeveloped countries. One of the men asked him what he found wrong with the churches of America.

Osborn's eyes got misty. He said, "When I come back from Africa and sit in an American church, I cry. Your music, even in the smallest American church, is a hundred times better than any church in Africa. Even the most uneducated American preacher preaches better than most African preachers. There is so much good in American churches that I can't find anything wrong."

It was one of the most refreshing statements I have ever heard.

A national leader told me that as he was on his way to speak to a group of pastors, the Lord spoke to him. "Only at the level you are able to love those with whom you disagree are you able to love Me."

Instead of exhorting the pastors, my friend got up and asked them to forgive him for his harsh judgments.

Revival broke out.

It's fun to throw rocks at crystal cathedrals, but our enemy is not inside the body. He does not live in Tulsa or Ft. Lauderdale. Our enemy is the devil, who is murdering and corrupting innocent lambs; defiling and deceiving struggling shepherds.

What, then, are the pollen and nectar that unify the battling tribes of bees? For tribal people we are, and tribal, it seems, we will remain. Is it not the Holy Spirit who unites? Then, as bees among the flowers, we return to the hive to make our joint deposit in the comb — that the kingdom may be blessed with honey.

Part Five

———

ON LIVING IN
THE KINGDOM

Twenty-six

A SCOUT'S HONOR

NO BOOK influenced my young life more than the Boy Scout handbook. In it I found a wonderful world of semaphore flags, sheepshanks, clove hitches, lean-tos and reflector ovens. It was my personal guidebook from the time I was twelve until I was sixteen. It took me from Tenderfoot, through the exciting world of merit badges, all the way to the coveted rank of Eagle Scout.

Youth activities in our little town — aside from a spitball fight in Sunday school or a Friday night dance — were nonexistent. Scouting was everything. In scouting I felt the tug toward manhood. Older boys discipled younger boys. Scoutmasters took us on camping and canoe trips. I learned how to apply a tourniquet and a splint, salute my superiors, have my uniform inspected and feel pride through hard-earned accomplishments.

As a scout I learned all the important concepts that would later make life rich and meaningful. I learned to relate to a small group in my patrol and troop. I learned to respect — not fear or destroy — nature. With only a hatchet, knife, rope and compass I could live in the wilderness. I learned Indian lore, loyalty and how to be part of a world brotherhood.

A Boy Scout loved God and country. He respected his parents.

He went to church. He believed in good deeds, loyalty, thrift, courage, physical fitness and — most of all — being prepared. I took a vow that I still try to uphold. *He must be prepared at any time to save life, help injured persons and share the home duties. He must do at least one "good turn" to somebody every day.*

But with the good times were times of disappointment — the same disappointment I have suffered in adult life and in my church.

It wasn't with scouting; it was with scouts. Particularly scout leaders.

One August afternoon five of us young teenagers headed for the girly show at the annual summer carnival on the fairgrounds.

The sideshow barker had gathered a small crowd of mostly teenage boys. Two tired, flabby women were gyrating on the platform in bathing suits. Inside, the barker told us, we could "see it all" for fifty cents. We gave each other knowing looks, told the ticket taker we were "of age" (we were all thirteen) and entered the semidark tent where scratchy Egyptian music was playing.

An old bump-and-grind woman came out on the tiny stage and began to strip. She finally got down to what I imagined was the fabled G-string. Then, in a whirl and a flash, it was gone. Before we could blink, she looked at us, threw her hips out and disappeared behind the drape. The show was over.

I felt dirty. It was the first time I had seen a naked woman. I felt degraded and, yes, cheated. I had wasted a week's allowance for a scar that would remain in my memory for a lifetime.

But the worst part was when we turned around to leave. There, in the back of the little tent, was our new scoutmaster. I knew we had been caught, yet inwardly I was relieved. I sensed I needed both punishment and help. Especially help. I didn't like what I had done and needed to be absolved. But the scoutmaster didn't see us in the dark tent. He had something else on his mind. Walking around the inside edge of the tent, he had found the other stripper and was talking to her in a hushed conversation.

We kept out of his sight, laughing quietly that we hadn't been caught — but had caught him instead. We got down on hands and knees and crawled under the edge of the tent into the hot Saturday afternoon sunlight.

Ordinarily I would have been excited by the midway: the music, the roar of the motorcycles in the pit, the whirling colors of the octopus and the tilt-a-whirl. But I was sick at my stomach. My technicolor world had turned to gray.

Overshadowing everything was a deep sense of moral revulsion — sadness — over the woman who had degraded herself in front of a bunch of teenage boys. From my father I had inherited quite a lofty concept of womanhood. I stood when a woman entered the room. I helped my mother or my sister with her chair at the table. To have spoken harshly to a woman, much less struck her, would have been a sin of the first magnitude. Now that pristine image of womanhood had been soiled by my first cheap glimpse of flesh — an image that remains in my mind even to this day.

Then there was the searing guilt. I had violated that deep sense of morality ingrained by the Boy Scout oath: *"On my honor I will do my best to do my duty to God and my country...to keep myself physically strong, mentally awake and morally straight."* I desperately needed forgiveness, absolution. But the only man who could give it, my scoutmaster, was still in the tent.

That, perhaps, was the deepest wound of all. I had seen the dark side of a man I looked to for light. As my scoutmaster he had been my hero, the bearer of the torch, the lifter of the standard. He was the man who challenged us to excel, to be noble, to do right. If I couldn't trust my scoutmaster, how could I ever be cleansed of my own sin?

It was my first introduction to life the way it really is — unfair and full of disappointments. But it prepared me for what I later discovered was truth. It is God who cleanses and absolves — not man. While scouts strive to be trustworthy, God alone can be trusted. My task is to forgive and love, for love covers a multitude of sins — even the sins of leaders.

Twenty-seven

THE ROACH BUSTERS

THERE WAS a message on my answering machine. Usually my secretary takes these off, but she was out, so I sat down and played back the tape. The accent was "down-South black," warm and comfortable, the kind I grew up hearing as I worked with my father's pickers in the Florida citrus groves.

"Mr. Buckingham, this is Willie in Baton Rouge. I'd sure like to talk to you." Then he left his number.

My secretary usually returns all calls from people I do not know. But there was something intriguing about this voice, something familiar. On impulse I called him back.

I know better than to attempt to imitate Willie Barrow's accent — especially on paper. He's too unique a character for that. But maybe I can impart his spirit.

"I talked to you more than a year ago," he said. "I was in bad shape, depressed, financially strapped, searching for answers."

Gradually it came back to me. I remembered this warm feeling I had the first time I talked to him, the deep impression that this was a special man of God.

"I'd just read one of your books," he reminded me. "I'd never called an author before, but I was desperate. You listened to me, then you prayed for me over the phone...." His voice broke.

"Ever since that time," he continued, "everything I've touched has turned to gold. I have to pinch myself to see if I'm dreaming, things are so good. I've become vice president of a chemical company. Among other things, we manufacture a remarkable roach spray. It's the finest roach poison ever invented. We're selling millions of cans each month. Last week a U.S. senator called, asking me to come to Washington, D.C., and kill all the roaches in the federal buildings."

"Watch out, Willie," I cautioned, "that could include half the Senate, the majority of the Supreme Court, the administration of the Post Office Department, the entire Small Business Administration — "

"No," he laughed back. "I mean real roaches. The kind that crawl around and spread germs."

Willie Barrow hadn't called me to hear me wisecrack about pork-barrel politics. He had called to thank me genuinely for praying for him — and because he had read that morning that Florida was having an invasion of roaches.

"That's right," I told him. "We've had killer bees from Brazil coming in from Miami, and now a new breed of roaches, the Asian roach, has come in through the Port of Tampa. They're heading toward the East Coast. Fortunately, they stopped over in Lakeland to attend Karl Strader's church and haven't gotten this far yet."

Florida has always had roaches. We have the crawling kind and the flying kind. We also have big things called palmetto bugs, which look like roaches but are twice as wide.

We also have spiders — millions of them of varying sizes and ferocity. Often as my wife, Jackie, and I lie in bed reading before going to sleep at night, she'll leap up, screaming and pointing at one of those huge "leaper" spiders, the size of a hand, crawling across the ceiling. Her screams — as she stands in the middle of the bed shouting, "Get him! Get him!" — are a signal for me to get up, plug in the hose to our central vacuum system, sneak up on the spider and suck it into the hose before it leaps into bed with us. It works great, but I keep wondering what's happening downstairs in that vacuum bag, which one day I'll have to empty. What strange mutations are occurring? Could we be breeding...(shudder)...it's best not to think about it.

Florida also has ants, crickets, mosquitoes, lizards, creeping things, crawling things, slithering things, hopping things, things that wiggle up your pants leg and things that fall off the ceiling and into your lap when you're sitting in your easy chair half asleep watching TV. Once a tiny scorpion fell off the ceiling in the middle of the night and stung my sleeping wife.

But most of all Florida has roaches. Especially this new Asian breed. Unlike the standard Florida roach, which can fly only four or five feet, the Asian model can fly 120 feet — or at least it seems to be that far. Earlier this year a roach count in a field in Lakeland revealed 100,000 to the acre. Roachologist Phil Koehler of the University of Florida says five females and one male can produce one hundred tons of roaches per year. Good grief! That's what an aircraft carrier weighs.

"Ever since I read that article I've been praying for you," Willie said. "I told the Lord, 'I've got this friend down in Florida, and he's gonna need help. What can I do?'

"Then the Lord said, 'Give him your gift.' So I'm sending you a case of my roach spray. Just one spraying in your home will kill all roaches up to four months. It's odorless and guaranteed to work overnight."

It arrived the next week. In two days every roach in our house was dead. It really is remarkable stuff. God has blessed Willie's company, and his roach spray can now be purchased in many hardware and grocery stores around the nation.

More important than getting rid of my roaches, however, I've gained a friend. I've yet to meet Willie Barrow face-to-face, but he calls occasionally just to bless me and to see if I'm roach-free.

All because I once took the time to pray over the phone for a stranger.

Twenty-eight

TRUTH AND CONSEQUENCE

THE STAFF members of a church I know have vowed among themselves never to listen to charges against any other person on the staff. If there are accusations, they insist that the accusing person talk directly to the person accused.

It sounds like a great policy for all of us, doesn't it — never to speak a bad word about someone else, especially behind his back? The problem with that particular creed, however, is that it is more Rotarian than biblical. Like it or not, we still need a "watchman on the wall."

Several years ago a man with a ministry behind the Iron Curtain asked me to write a book about his co-worker who had supposedly escaped from Eastern Europe. But as we talked, some things did not ring true. I sent a cable to a trusted friend in Holland. Could he shed any light on the situation? He responded with a one-sentence telegram: "I don't like to say bad things about a brother in the Lord."

It was enough.

My Dutch friend could have gone into detail — dirty details. But rather than defame a man's character he simply warned me to stay away. I dropped the entire matter. Later newspaper disclosures about this same man indicated I made a wise decision.

The issue remains, however. Whenever one writes (or speaks) about real people involved in real events, how far does one go? How much does one reveal?

I'm having to face this question in writing my newsletter, the *Buckingham Report*. It's an insider's report to Christian leaders. How much do you tell, even to those who have a need to know? When does truth become gossip?

Shortly before Kathryn Kuhlman died she asked me to write her autobiography. "Wait until after I'm gone," she said, "then tell it all for the glory of God."

Kathryn knew I was not a muckraker or a sensationalist. At the same time she had a regard for truth and realized that lasting good comes only when all facts are revealed. She also knew that when I sat down to write *Daughter of Destiny* I would realize it is the truth which makes us free, not just the facts.

The Kathryn Kuhlman Foundation, which carried on after her death, hired an attorney to try to stop publication of the book. They contended that the public did not have the right to know many of the things I included.

Legally I was OK. The courts have ruled that eminent people — "public figures" such as Kathryn Kuhlman — are more or less fair game as long as the writer does not display "actual malice." That means the writer must not show a "reckless disregard for the truth." The foundation argued that some things should never be revealed. I took a position that if God chose to reveal King David's sordid sexual life and the apostle Paul's hot temper, why should today's servants of God enjoy higher privilege?

There is a thin line between muckraking and solid analysis. It is called *love*. It is love that enables a communicator to draw the line between the sordid exposé and truth revealed without malice.

Here's my dilemma: I believe Christians should know what's going on. They have a right to know — indeed a responsibility to know — and this responsibility often transcends the right to privacy. I believe that anything built on less than truth will ultimately fail.

I am one of those who believes that the framers of the Bill of Rights heard God when they insisted on freedom of the press. I have been in too many nations where the newspapers and magazines reported only what the government wanted. I believe the *Washington Post* did us all a great service by revealing the rottenness of the Nixon administration. A people kept in ignorance are a people who walk in darkness.

But we must remember: It is not facts which make us free, but truth. Nowhere is that more important than in the kingdom of God. Yet in this dimension we operate on different principles from those of the worldly press. Here even truth must be tempered by love. For instance, I am not telling you the name of the Iron Curtain minister. It would be of no benefit for you to know his name. Besides, I would be planting a seed of distrust in your mind, making it difficult for you to accept him if he does repent and change.

In other words, knowing facts, especially negative facts, about someone is an awesome responsibility. The *fact* is, the fellow is a scoundrel. The *truth* is, God can change him. Facts, like a loaded gun, must be handled with great caution, for they can maim the innocent as well as the evildoer.

Facts are hard, objective. Truth is subjective. It involves facts but goes far beyond to reasons — and results. Newspapers operate without feelings. If it's fact, they print it. But truth involves feelings and morality. Its purpose is more than revelation — it is redemption.

The Christian communicator — journalist or preacher — knows there are times when publishing a story can harm or ruin someone's life. On the other hand, to refrain from revealing falsehood can be even more damaging. The secret is doing it without rancor, without exhibiting the "gotcha" spirit which is so evident in little people who think the fastest way to the top is to pull down the big guys.

Someone asked, "Well, how would you feel if someone talked about your dark side and revealed all the scandal in your life?" That's not a problem for me. I determined some time ago to beat everyone else to the punch through self-revelation. And to be repentant if caught in some ungodly act. Confession — along with a teachable spirit — remains the best policy.

But until we reach that point, God will no doubt continue to commission others to pull down our icons, prick our balloons and (with love, I hope) call us to honesty.

Twenty-nine

BIBLES BOUND IN SHOE LEATHER

I THOUGHT the fighting had died down, but it seems the evangelicals are still shooting at each other over the question of whether the Bible is "inerrant" or merely "inspired." It seems to me, though, that unless the Word of God is transferred from book to heart, the question of inerrancy is meaningless. It all came to mind this last week when I was cleaning out my bookcase and found an old Bible with the pages half missing and the cover chewed away by roaches. The sensible thing was to throw it away, but somehow it didn't seem right to drop a Bible in the trash can.

Everyone knows how to get rid of an old flag. But so far no one has come up with a set of rules on how to dispose of an old Bible. A different man, one whose roots do not extend back into a Baptist Sunday school, probably could have tossed it into the trash can without a second thought. But this was the Bible I received when I was promoted from the primary department to the junior department. Besides, it was a genuine King James Version — the "inerrant" one. I wound up putting it back on the shelf — tattered cover and all. I just couldn't bring myself to toss it into the garbage compactor along with the used coffee grounds.

In the fall of 1982 when a former running back with the Miami

Dolphins was arrested for selling cocaine, the TV cameras showed him entering the courtroom holding a Bible in his hand-cuffed hands. I never did find out whether he believed in iner-rancy, plenary inspiration or just plain good luck. But none of that seemed to impress the judge. It seems the sale of dope to kids spoke louder than a man carrying a Bible to court. The unfortu-nate man wound up being sentenced to prison for more than twenty years — Bible and all.

Back when I was involved in pastoral counseling there were always certain people who, when they came to my office, brought their Bible. They never opened it during the counseling session, but sitting there with the Bible in their lap seemed to make them feel better.

A friend of mine means it when he says he never goes out of the house without his "sword." Lately he's been coming down hard on his wife because she only carries a New Testament. Even though it has an olive wood cover and was purchased in the Holy Land, he's still not satisfied. "That's not a sword. It's only a dag-ger."

Yet when Paul speaks of the "sword of the Spirit" which he says is the "word of God," I don't think he's talking about a *Thompson Chain Reference Bible*. After all, his letter to the Ephe-sians was written 337 years before the Council of Carthage rati-fied the New Testament canon.

A lot of us grew up equating "thy word have I hid in my heart" with Scripture memorization. While all the Scripture is God's Word, God's Word is certainly more than Scripture — and was here long before it appeared on paper. When David wrote about God's Word being a lamp to his feet, he was not talking about the Bible — but about Jesus Christ. The same is true with Isaiah, who said the grass withers and the flower fades, but the Word of the Lord abides forever — and that's more than a brown calfskin book published by A. J. Holman. The need today is not more Bibles in top-grained cowhide, but Bibles in shoe leather. Too many of us have been left bleeding after being thumped over the head with a Bible — carried by some argumentative repre-sentative of sectarian religion who knows the words but has never had an experience with the Word. These religious terrorists prowl the world with their quivers full of sharpened proof texts, shooting at all who disagree — in the holy name of Jesus.

Frankly, I'd rather be around some illiterate who never will be able to pronounce "Mephibosheth" and spends half the sermon time trying to look up the Book of Paul — but has a heart full of godly love — than some Bible-quoting scribe who never has let the words of God become the Word of God.

I love my Bible. I am grateful for those who teach it, envious of those who memorize it and respectful of those who translate it and spread its good news of salvation. But there is a tendency — whenever we write "holy" on a thing — to venerate it. The Bible is holy in that it is different; but it is to be used, not worshipped.

We have friends who won't allow their grandchildren in the house because they might dirty the carpets. We have other friends who treat the Bible like the Israelites treated the ark of the covenant. Like the sons of Eli, they are unable to transfer holy Scripture into holy living. They, too, are Ichabod.

The Bible is not a lucky rabbit's foot. Carrying it to church — or to court — is not enough. It must be translated into our lives. Having written this, I returned to my bookcase. I took that battered old Bible and dropped it tenderly into the trash can. Bookcase Bibles — even if they are inerrant — are worthless. Only the Word of the Lord abides forever.

Thirty

LEGACY

S HORTLY AFTER my dad became a Christian, at age sixty-two, he began looking around for things he could give away. Although he had been successful in his Florida business and in citrus agriculture, and had accumulated many things, giving became more important than getting. He spent the last twenty-six years of his life giving things away. He once told me his goal was to be like Job, also a successful businessman, who left this world as he entered it — owning nothing.

He came close to meeting that goal.

The afternoon after he died, at the age of eighty-seven, I went through his remaining possessions. Everything was within reach of his bed — either on or in his little nightstand. He had been wearing most of his clothes: a pair of khaki pants, a tan dress shirt, a black bow tie and a pair of fuzzy white socks. He also owned two other pairs of socks, two sets of underwear and a pair of pajamas. On top of the nightstand were his dollar pocket watch, glasses, a soft hairbrush and his worn, dog-eared Bible. His final possession was a narrow-bladed grapefruit knife, which he loved to pull from his pocket in the citrus grove to show us kids how to peel a grapefruit in a circular fashion so the peeling never broke.

He indeed left as he arrived — owning virtually nothing.

Other possessions — house, properties and money — had been given away before he died. I suspect what he inherited in heaven, apart from his salvation, was in direct proportion to what he gave on earth.

He had been very direct with his five grown children. He would wisely give money when needed — when we were getting started in life and career. But he was specific — there would be no money for us in his will. He left an inheritance to take care of our mother [editor's note: who now at ninety-five is continuing to use it]. But he knew that money or property left to children often divides families. All his possessions — and they were considerable — had been given ahead of time or were willed to the churches and mission organizations he believed in and loved.

We kids agreed. It was his money, and he was following God's direction. He had given us college educations, helped us in times of need and blessed us with an example that continues to change our lives.

His initial experience with Jesus — which started this change — came during a time of personal anguish and shame. I had just graduated from high school and had done something that embarrassed the family. Consequently, he felt he had failed as a father.

In deep despair he left the house one October afternoon in 1950 and walked into the citrus grove on the back side of the property. Kneeling between two big grapefruit trees, he cried — and God came rushing to meet him in great and powerful glory.

Daddy had been a churchgoer all his life. He had taught the men's class in the local Methodist church for many years. After he met Jesus, the Bible became his most prized possession. Prior to this he had never read anything but the ancient King James Version. But the week after his born-again experience he purchased a copy of J. B. Phillips's new translation of Paul's epistles, one of the first modern-language translations. It was the beginning of a love affair with the Bible that lasted until the day he laid the written Word aside and entered the Writer's study.

Fifteen years after his conversion I went through my own "dark night of the soul." My sense of personal failure overwhelmed me. I had failed as a minister, a father and a husband. I went to see my dad in Florida. He told me of his own spiritual pilgrimage, then took me out behind the house and showed me that spot between the two grapefruit trees.

At the end of my visit he reached up on the shelf of his study and gave me his much-marked copy of the Phillips translation. A prized possession.

I took it with me, intrigued over my dad's underlines. I didn't have to read far. In the preface the translator wrote of his own spiritual struggle with radical Christianity. Daddy had underlined Phillips's conclusion: *"Perhaps if we believed what they (those early Christians) believed, we might achieve what they achieved."*

In the margin my father had written, "Aha!"

That sentence, which had started my father's search for spiritual power, now started mine. It climaxed a year later with a life-changing baptism in the Holy Spirit.

What a wonderful legacy.

Thirty-one

ANOTHER MAN'S SERVANT

WHEN MISSIONARIES visit the States and see our opulence, they can't help but contrast it to the poverty they've just left.

But poverty, and riches, are relative. I have two cars. I live in a two-story brick house. I can buy anything I want within reason. I've never known hunger. What should I do when confronted with the poverty of the Third World?

I'll tell you what I have done. I loan my cars to missionaries when they are home on furlough — and I buy the gas and pay the repair bills. My house stays filled with people in need of ministry. I give a large percentage of my income to support those in ministry and to feed the poor. Ten years ago Jackie and I moved out of a small subdivision to our present house on twenty acres in a semi-rural setting. By today's standards we got it at a steal — including the guest cottage. But for five years both of us lived with a deep-seated guilt because we had such a nice place. That has passed. I simply see my purchase as a wise move. I no longer believe God condemns prosperity. Indeed, I think He desires it for us — as long as we use what we have for His glory.

On the other hand, I, too, am appalled by what is going on in some sectors of Western Christendom. Extravagance grieves me.

Yet, extravagance is relative to culture. Recently I helped deliver an evaporative cooler to a Christian Indian living in a dirt-floored, two-room hut in the Mexican desert. That provided him — and the ten people in his tiny house — a degree of comfort. But in the eyes of his neighbors it was sheer extravagance.

I admire the way Sen. John D. "Jay" Rockefeller IV approached his job as a volunteer in the antipoverty program in Appalachia some years ago. Rockefeller, one of the richest men in the world, took his bride, the daughter of millionaire Sen. Charles Percy, to Emmons, West Virginia (population, two hundred), as a Peace Corps worker.

"I took slides with me," Rockefeller said. "I gathered everyone in the community center, and I showed slides of my family, my house, my car, my father, how I lived. I said, 'This is who I am, and I am here to help you. I come from a world that may be different, but you'll find me serious and caring and wanting to help.' " Those grateful people later elected him governor — then U.S. senator.

That, it seems, put riches in the right perspective.

What has God told me to do? He's told me to withhold judgment from His servants — to be kind, tenderhearted and forgiving — even if I do not understand.

For instance, God did not tell me to build a splendid university as He told Oral Roberts. But I'm glad Oral obeyed, and I've sent him four of my five children to educate.

I've looked but I cannot find a single biblical injunction to tear down what others are doing in the name of Jesus. My call? To use the things I control to God's glory — and allow my brothers to answer to God for the things they control.

Once I spent a week in a Catholic monastery with about fifty of the nation's charismatic leaders. We were miles apart in doctrine. Some were classic Pentecostals. Some were liberals. Several were Catholic priests. We spent all week listening to each other.

At night, when we finished with the day's activities, we went down to the kitchen for snacks. Some drank beer, some lemonade. One afternoon I listened to a devoted Catholic scholar tell how Mary encouraged him to love and worship Jesus. The week did not change my doctrine, but it softened my spirit.

I wish some of my friends who are so critical of Catholics would take a week each year, as I do, getting to know these men and listening to their hearts. Perhaps they would come away as I do, realizing God is bigger than our interpretation of the Bible and that all men who are committed to the lordship of Jesus Christ are brothers.

As I examine my past critical attitude of the life-styles and doctrines of others, I realize most of it has come from secondhand knowledge. Recently I sat in a minister's conference in Tulsa and heard Kenneth Copeland preach. I'd never cared for Copeland's approach, but, again, I'd never heard him in person. That night I left the room a mellowed man.

Who is right? One who drives a luxury automobile and whose ostentation seems second only to the Taj Mahal, or my missionary friend who drives a battered car over rocky Argentine roads and wears threadbare clothes? Who is right?

I suspect, when earth's last picture is painted, that the bright lights here at home will blend right into the dusty colors painted by my missionary friends, and somehow the picture will come out looking just the way God intended.

Thirty-two

PRAYING FOR THE DOA

LAST YEAR I spent three weeks in the uttermost part of the earth — the Indonesian province of Irian Jaya.

Located on the western half of the island of New Guinea, Irian Jaya is nearly all jungle with less than a hundred miles of roads in the province — an area twice the size of the state of Georgia. The last leg of my flight was in a single-engine plane over two hundred miles of impenetrable jungle to a tiny airstrip hacked out of the trees.

While at the missionary compound, I read a survey report submitted by a team of translators who had just discovered a never-before-known tribe of people. These tribal people — who called themselves "Doa" — lived on a shallow river hundreds of miles from the nearest settlement.

A Wycliffe pilot had spotted their tiny village while flying over an uncharted section of the jungle. Later a two-man linguistic survey team from Wycliffe set out to try to contact the villagers. The men traveled several days in a dugout canoe up the winding jungle river. When the river became impassable because of rocks and logs, they carried their canoe through the snake-infested jungle until they could put it back in the water. They finally located the tribe.

The Doa people had no alphabet and no written language and had never seen a white man. Their entire tribal population was less than three hundred. They stayed alive by hunting with bows and arrows and fishing in the river.

Tragically, they had never heard about God.

"When can you send a translation team to the Doa people?" I asked Dick Hugonoit, director of Wycliffe's Indonesia branch.

"It will be years," he said. "There are more than two hundred tribes in Indonesia. They all speak different languages. We are working in only seventeen of those. The Doas will have to wait."

When I returned to the States, I couldn't shake my burden to intercede for them.

I wrote Wycliffe Bible Translators headquarters in Huntington Beach, California, to ask if anyone was praying on a regular basis for the Doas. Wycliffe has a program whereby one can write, obtain the name of some Bibleless tribe someplace in the world (there are thirty-six hundred tribes like the Doas all over the world) and agree to pray for them until someone takes them the Word of God. [For more information, contact Wycliffe at P.O. Box 2727, Huntington Beach, CA 92647; (714) 969-4600.]

A Wycliffe representative, Betty Baptista, wrote back that no one was praying for the Doas. She sent me a little card which I taped on the wall next to my word processor to remind me to pray daily. The card read: "I am praying daily for the Doa people of Irian Jaya until they have God's Word in their own language." It was accompanied by a verse of Scripture from Psalm 65:2 (KJV): "O thou that hearest prayer, unto thee shall all flesh come."

I confess I was both excited and frightened over this commitment. I had never prayed for a tribe of people — especially people I didn't know. Then there was the factor of *daily* prayer. Could I discipline myself to pray every day?

Every morning when I come into my study I turn on my word processor. After I turn on the machine, it takes about thirty seconds to boot up — that is, to load my program into the computer. Normally that is dead time. I just sit there each morning while my disk drive whirs, rattles and whines, waiting for the monitor screen to light up and indicate it is ready for me to go to work. Since the card was next to my computer, I decided to use those thirty seconds to pray for the Doas.

But something happened. Each morning as I prayed during

that boot-up time, I began to receive little visions. I could picture those little grass huts on the sandbar along the river. In my mind's eye I could see the brown-skinned people wandering around the tiny village. Children were playing along the river. Women were working with the materials their men brought in from the jungle. Men with bows and long arrows were roaming the jungle or paddling their dugout canoes in search of food.

Then I saw them afraid at night — afraid of the demons, afraid of the snakes and crocodiles, afraid of the dark. I could see the witch doctor trying to use his power to hold back the spiritual darkness. On several occasions I actually began to cry as I prayed for those unknown people — lost and without hope. Often my thirty-second prayer time went to five, sometimes ten minutes.

I asked God to send them a Bible translator who would move into their village, learn their language, translate the Bible and teach them to read the Word of God.

Six months later I was in California to speak to the combined boards of Wycliffe. We were meeting in a retreat center in the high mountains above Los Angeles. During one of my sessions I mentioned I was praying for the Doa people.

At the close of that session, one of the board members who had just arrived from Indonesia came forward. He was excited. "Just last week," he said, "Peter and Mary Jane Munnings, Wycliffe members from Canada now living in Irian Jaya, entered the Doa village as translators. They were years ahead of schedule, but word came that the Doas wanted someone to move into their village and live with them in order to translate the Bible. And...the Munnings 'just happened' to be available."

To my knowledge I was the only one in the world praying for the Doa people. That left little doubt as to whose prayer God answered.

Now I have a second card taped to the wall next to my card for the Doa people. It is to remind me to pray for Peter and Mary Jane Munnings — whom I have never met. But since they are helping my friends the Doas, they need my prayer support also.

God is answering everyone's prayers these days.

Thirty-three

I WAS SCARED.
I DIDN'T GO.

IN MARCH 1975 I received an impassioned plea from an *ad hoc* committee of missionaries in South Vietnam. The letter was written and signed by a Christian and Missionary Alliance missionary representing a large number of missionaries from many denominations.

It said, in essence, "The communists have started their final push, and it is now obvious we are going to have to leave. The sad part is, all we've worked for and accomplished so far will be destroyed when we pull out. The communists will burn the Bibles we leave behind; they will turn the church buildings into communist meeting halls; they will take over our hospitals; they will disband the churches and kill the pastors. There is nothing we can leave behind which will have a lasting effect.

"As we prayed together and searched the Scripture, we have discovered Jesus faced a similar situation when He left earth to return to heaven. He did not leave anything behind. No church buildings, no Bibles, no trained pastors. All He left was His Holy Spirit.

"We are writing to ask if you are willing to come to Vietnam and impart to us the same gift Jesus imparted to His disciples, that we might in turn give this gift to those we are going to have to leave behind?"

There was more, but that was the literal essence of the letter.

I didn't know how to respond.

Our church was small at the time and did not have the money to send me. The publishing company I worked for was on the skids and had no money. Even if I had been able to come up with the money, there was another factor looming over me. I was afraid to go. This was a time when tens of thousands of people were fleeing Vietnam. It didn't make sense for me to go there. And possibly die there.

I knew of three missionaries who had been killed in Vietnam. Just the year before I had met the young widow of a Bible translator who had been gunned down by the Vietcong. I had heard reports of others having been captured and tortured.

I waited another week, but the conclusion was inevitable. I knew I had no choice but to go. I could charge my ticket on my credit card. If I didn't come back, someone else could pay the bill.

On Easter Sunday I cabled the mission group at DaNang, accepting their invitation and asking for directions. Tuesday morning I picked up the paper. DaNang had fallen. The nation was in chaos. My cable had been too late. Within three weeks it was all over.

Since then I have talked to several who were part of the group who issued the invitation. All have tried to absolve me of guilt by saying their letter was sent too late. They, too, had put off asking. The prospect of changing their theology, requesting an experience they didn't even believe in (the baptism in the Holy Spirit), was a tough decision, even in the face of death. But eventually they were forced to drop their traditions, cling to truth and ask God to give them the only thing Jesus gave His disciples — the gift of the Holy Spirit.

That episode in my life drove me into a period of deep introspection. Out of it came several positive things. One was a determination to define my purpose in life. I needed to know exactly *why* God had put me on earth. I suspected my fear had come out of confusion of purpose rather than the mere desire for self-preservation. But I would never know that until I had some kind of definition of purpose.

In good editorial fashion I decided to boil that purpose down to one sentence.

It was simple: to impart the Holy Spirit to the generation in which I live.

Having determined that (and I am not so cocky as to believe purposes do not change, so I keep going back about every six months to see if the cloud has moved), I finally understood the motive behind those men mentioned in Revelation 12:11: "They overcame him by the blood of the Lamb and by the word of their testimony; they did not love their lives so much as to shrink from death."

Once you know who you are and why you're here, there's no need to be afraid. All God requires of us is faithfulness. Our times are in His hands.

I determined, back then, not to make safety, comfort or money a standard on which I made decisions for the Lord. If God wanted me to go someplace no one else would go, I would accept.

That decision has cost me dearly across the years. It has also allowed me to be in the midst of some of the most exciting events since Pentecost.

I've just returned from another of those experiences in what is quite literally earth's uttermost part — the steaming jungles of the Indonesian state of Irian Jaya. Stay tuned. Now I want to share what I learned in the heart of that dense, snake-infested jungle.

Thirty-four

THEIR ROADS
JUST STOP

I RIAN JAYA is — quite literally — earth's uttermost part. Lying six degrees south of the equator in the South Pacific, it makes up the western half of the island of New Guinea. Even the Indonesian travel brochure stuck in the seat pocket of the Garuda Airlines described it as "primitive" with "extreme heat in the snake-infested jungles."

It took a full week of travel for me to get there from my comfortable home in Florida. I went there because I was summoned by God and by the Indonesian branch of Wycliffe Bible Translators. I was to speak three times a day for eight days at the annual Bible conference for the 120 missionaries who had come together at the jungle camp from all over Indonesia.

Kipling once wrote of a place where the roads run out and stop. That literally happens at Jaya Pura, the provincial capital. From there it is still 120 miles over the top of the jungle to the little mission base of Danau Bira. It is accessible only by helicopter or small plane piloted by a jungle pilot.

The ministry was intense. These young couples did not leave America to rear their children in the midst of a place like this on a lark. They had no time for game-playing. They were literally offering their lives to get a job done — translating the Word of God into the language of tribal people, many of whom have never seen a white face before. When I arrived with my message about the power of the Holy Spirit, they drank it in thirstily. There was no time to debate silly theological issues. The time was too critical.

These are mostly young people, under thirty-five. Tough and dedicated, they are nevertheless subject to great discouragement. And they are constantly under the attack of Satan — whose power is stronger in the Indonesian jungles than any place I have ever encountered him.

My last afternoon in Irian Jaya we had flown in from the jungle to spend the night at Sentani, on the coast where Gen. Douglas MacArthur had launched his assault against the Japanese to reclaim the Philippines. The missionary we were staying with told us matter-of-factly of the witch doctor in his tribal allocation who had the power to call a certain killer crocodile out of the jungle river and dispatch him into a local village to seek out and eat the child of someone who had been cursed by another villager.

I'm not accustomed to encounters with this kind of demon power. Back home I'm around folks who are casting out demons of nail-biting and, on rare occasions, a "denominational" spirit.

The entire scene was unreal. It was like a visit into hell with a group of Christians determined to pluck men and women from the flames. Just being in their presence made me want to take off my shoes. And I would have done it had I not been afraid to step on a death adder along the jungle trail — as often happens to the Indians.

There are between two hundred and three hundred separate Indian tribes in Irian Jaya alone. All practice demon worship. One afternoon I sat with a group of Bauzi Indians at a great feast. They had slaughtered three pigs, buried them in a pit with hot stones and jungle vegetables, and called their friends to join them. I watched as the women, with a baby at one breast and a puppy at the other, tore open the pit with their strong feet so the men could serve the food. There was singing and dancing — but it was without joy. The anthropologists complain that the missionaries are ruining the Indians' "pristine" existence. But there is nothing pristine about being under the control of Satan.

One of these atheistic anthropologists who had been such a staunch opponent of the missionaries, a government official told me, fled in terror when the word came that an Indian had put a curse on her and there was a possibility the crocodile was coming for her that night.

No one in the jungle doubts the necessity of being filled with the Holy Spirit. Except fools and Pharisees.

All this is still very fresh in my mind as I start thinking about buying Christmas gifts for my family and friends. How, I am asking myself, can I in good conscience spend my money on gadgets when I remember the jungle pilot who looked at my ragged old jogging shoes so longingly. To buy a pair like them in Indonesia — in his size — would cost seventy-five dollars. I gave him mine even though they were a half size too small.

So what do I do for Christmas when all I can do is remember those young couples out there in the jungles rearing their children among the death adders and cobras, doing daily battle against the powers of darkness — for the sake of Jesus.

Who says there are no heroes left? The question is — will I honor them, or will I continue as usual, spending my money on myself?

Part Six

———

ON DISAGREEING, BUT WITHOUT BEING DISAGREEABLE

Thirty-five

ACCUSING
THE BRETHREN

FEW THINGS bring more terror to a small child than listening to his parents verbally abuse each other. When sides are drawn, the child is caught in an untenable situation. This is especially true when one or both parents draw the child into the argument, forcing him to take sides.

"If you love me you'll leave your father."

"Your mom is crazy. Don't pay any attention to her."

The child, however, loves both parents. He needs both parents. Even if the child has enough discernment to figure out one parent is right and the other wrong, how can he turn his back on someone he loves?

It is this situation in which many of us now find ourselves. For reasons known only to God, some popular Christian leaders have taken their disagreements to the public — the unbelieving public — and the children are confused.

When King Saul was caught in horrible sin and ended his life on his sword, a saddened King David warned his soldiers: "Tell it not in Gath, proclaim it not in the streets of Ashkelon, lest the daughters of the Philistines be glad..." (2 Sam. 1:20).

Oral Roberts's unique approach to fund raising several years ago became caustic fodder for the cannons of every columnist in the nation. Mike Royko of the *Chicago Tribune* said he was praying Roberts would die. Doonesbury began a countdown to Roberts's death date. None of them mentioned the cause for which Roberts was raising money: to provide free tuition so every graduate of the ORU medical school could spend at least four years as a medical missionary to Third World nations.

But we expected that from the public media.

A while back the *Washington Post*, in a front-page article, sneered at the fund-raising techniques used by John Meares in his Evangel Cathedral in Washington, D.C. The article quoted several "former members" who scoffed because Meares had encouraged his nearly all-black congregation to believe God for extra funds so they could build a new church building. Buried in the text was the purpose of the new building: to draw white members and work toward racial reconciliation. No reference was made that Meares, perhaps more than any other white man in America, has dedicated his life to bringing the gospel to inner-city blacks.

The world's media channels will never be fair.

However, when well-known Christian leaders use the airwaves — even if it's on "Christian" TV — to condemn other Christians, the children are confused.

One thing is sure: God is cleaning up His church. The Jim Bakker/Jimmy Swaggart/Marvin Gorman/Richard Dortch/John Ankerberg/Jerry Falwell debacle is vivid evidence. As the stories were breaking, God warned me to stay clear. "There are cracks at the bases of these modern towers which reach toward heaven," He said. "I am bringing them down." He went on to say He had "loosed the press," as He loosed the locusts on the Israelites (see Joel 1:4), for justice begins at the house of God.

"God is lancing a boil," Oral Roberts told me during a visit with him in his prayer tower. "Let the matter seethe."

On my way home I prayed, "What should I do?"

I heard God say: "The locusts will devour the fields of the just and the unjust. Therefore, stand with your friends until the shaking is over. The glory of the Lord will be your rear guard."

Recently I met with a group of longtime friends who gather annually to brainstorm issues and ideas. As always, our conversation drifted to a certain Christian community which some feel is heretical. As we talked I realized we had become a nest of negativism. "We never say anything good about these people," I blurted. "All we do is talk about them behind their backs."

The room became strangely silent. I felt bad, but we had fallen into the trap of the enemy. Satan is the "accuser of the brethren." When we join that chorus, we're playing on the wrong team. We wound up repenting and praying for our brothers.

What should we do when we cannot tolerate a brother's method?

Matthew 18 outlines the procedure. Jesus says disagreements between brothers should be handled with face-to-face confrontation "just between the two of you." If that does not settle the matter, take along an arbitrator. If the problem remains, it should come before the elders or a presbytery. (The Bible says to "tell it to the church." The term *ekklesia* refers to a small group of officials who represent the body.) At no place does He say, "Call a press conference."

Jesus equates lack of agreement with "binding" and agreement with "loosing." Disagreements spring from a controlling spirit, one that demands others agree with our life-style, our doctrine, our interpretation of the Bible. The controlling spirit binds, while the Spirit of Jesus looses. Jesus says that if two on earth *agree*, "it will be done for you by my Father in heaven. For where two or three *come together* in my name, there am I with them" (Matt. 18:19, italics added).

"Come together" refers to men who were once in disagreement but have worked through their problems using His procedure, laid down their right to be right and started treating each other as brothers.

There are those of us willing to form a presbytery and mediate such a meeting — even now — between these disagreeing brethren. Perhaps then the locusts will go home, and the children will sleep well at night.

Thirty-six

THE RETURN OF THE HERESY HUNTERS

J UST WHEN I had begun to believe it was safe to think out loud again, the heresy hunters returned.

I had hoped, once the controversial *The Seduction of Christianity* had slunk back into the murky depths where all back-listed books go to die, that the flurry of heresy hunting would subside.

Not so! It's not safe to go back into the water. The sharks have once again raised their ugly fins. Jaws has returned — and has brought his vicious brothers with him.

In November 1987 *Moody Monthly*, the flagship magazine of fundamentalist Christians, ran an article subtitled "An Update on Trends in Heretical and Cultic Religious Movements." The article listed all the old standby bad boys — Mormons, Moonies, Hare Krishnas, Jehovah's Witnesses. This time, though, they added a new heretic: the United Pentecostal Church.

The United Pentecostal Church?

"In an effort to appear Christian," *Moody Monthly* says, "sects such as...the United Pentecostal Church (...which deny the Trinity) hide behind their claim to be 'born-again Christians.' "

Branding the UPC as "heretics," the magazine says, "Probably the third largest pseudo-Christian sect in the world is the United Pentecostal Church, the largest group that teaches the 'oneness' heresy. Better known as the 'Jesus only' doctrine, it claims that Jesus is the Father, Son and Holy Spirit."

My UPC friends, who disdain the term "Jesus only," tell me they really do believe in the trinity. They just don't believe like the folks in Chicago.

The first heresy hunters were members of the ancient tribe of Manasseh, called Gileadites. There had been a long-standing feud between them and the Ephraimites in northern Israel. Determined to protect themselves from infiltrators, the Gileadites set up a checkpoint at the fords of the Jordan. They challenged anyone trying to cross the river to say the password: "shibboleth." Try as they could, the Ephraimites simply couldn't pronounce the word. It always came out "sibboleth." When that happened, the renegade Gileadites would cut off their heads.

Over the centuries the church has maintained its shibboleths. Ironically, the UPC is one of the most notorious when it comes to double-checking doctrinal credentials.

Last month a visitor in our church accosted me after a morning service, demanding to know if I baptized "only in the name of Jesus, according to Acts 19:5."

I told him the last person I baptized had been in the ocean, and I had done it in the name of Jesus only. He hugged me, called me "brother" and left. I didn't have the heart to tell him that I had intended to say "Father, Son and Holy Spirit" as found in Matthew 28:19 but had been knocked over by a huge wave just as I lowered the man into the water. The best I could do was scream, "Jesus!"

I guess that makes me "Jesus only."

Today's heresy hunters still use shibboleths. Fundamentalists, spotting an approaching political candidate, shout, "Say, 'prayer in public school.' " If you stammer even the slightest, off comes your head. At least one presidential candidate hired a Pentecostal preacher to coach him on how to pronounce evangelical words so he wouldn't slip up and say "sibboleth" as he courted the pastors of large churches.

Recently, however, the Gileadites got themselves elected to the Sanhedrin. Now heresy hunting is back in vogue, and Southern Baptists have been chopping heads. Home missionaries have been told if they speak in tongues they may lose their jobs. At least one seminary president resigned because he couldn't pronounce "inerrancy." Every time he was challenged it came out "inspiration." When I was growing up, all you had to believe about the Bible, to be a good Baptist, was that it was inspired.

Since I don't understand the trinity, I asked five different theologians to explain it to me. Each gave me a different explanation. That means we're all heretics. At least everyone but me.

When I think of the theology of my UPC brethren, I recall columnist George Will's story of a British member of Parliament who, coming down off the podium after delivering a comprehensive speech, asked Prime Minister Balfour, "How did I do, Arthur?"

"Splendidly, Henry, splendidly."

"Did you understand me, Arthur?"

"Not a word, Henry, not a word."

It's been a long time since the days of Huss, Wycliffe and Joan of Arc, and even though I don't understand "trinitarian" theology, the United Pentecostal Church gives class to today's sorry lot of accused heretics. If I were going to the stake I'd be honored to be tied up with them.

But if you ask me to say "shibboleth," stand back. Every time I try, I spit.

Thirty-seven

CHRISTIANS IN COURT MAKE SAD SPECTACLES

I S IT right for Christians to sue each other in secular court?

In West Virginia a pastor recently sued the church which voted him out. The jury was unable to reach a decision, and the judge declared a mistrial.

In a reversal of that, a group of Tennessee church members sued the pastor of their Baptist church, claiming he had stolen their church building by leading the rest of the people into "un-Baptistic" doctrine. In that case a non-Christian judge was forced to rule on what constitutes Baptist doctrine — and sided with the traditionalists.

The secular media loved it. To them it was more proof we Christians are simply a group of bumbling, fighting ignoramuses.

Last year a former member of our church, who had moved to another city, served papers on another church member, claiming he had defrauded her in a business deal. I wrote her, agreeing she had been wronged, but asking her to withdraw her civil suit and settle the matter through Christian mediation. Influenced by her non-Christian lawyer, she refused.

The judge ruled in her favor, granting her thirty thousand dollars. The defendant, unable to pay, went into bankruptcy. She received absolutely nothing except a lot of unfavorable newspaper publicity — and a bill from her lawyer for twenty-four thousand dollars.

Recently, a friend in another state was accused of slander by a charismatic preacher. My friend said his remarks were not slander — they were truth. He said he was willing to stand trial, but only before a court convened by the church and devoid of publicity. He agreed to abide by whatever decision the church court reached — even if it meant paying financial damages.

The accusing brother refused. He didn't want justice; he wanted revenge. So the matter wound up in secular court — and in the newspapers.

Who wins? Lawyers surely. They get the money. And Satan primarily. He always gets the victory when Christians disobey God and sue each other in secular court.

God realizes Christians are not perfect — that we will have disputes. Recognizing these imperfections, He had His servant Paul give specific instructions on how Christians should settle disputes.

The command is clear: "If any of you has a dispute with another, dare he take it before the ungodly for judgment instead of before the saints?...Therefore, if you have disputes about such matters, appoint as judges even men of little account in the church" (1 Cor. 6:1,4).

A short while ago two men in our church had a serious dispute. One, a dentist, contracted with a Christian builder to remodel his house. The men were longtime friends. But when the house was complete and the builder submitted his bill, the fire that fell was not the Pentecostal variety.

According to the dentist, the builder had overcharged him seven thousand dollars.

The builder suggested the dentist should fill a few more teeth and pay up.

The dentist asked the builder how he'd like to lose some teeth — right then.

The builder said, "I'll see you in court."

After the smoke cleared, both men realized they had an insoluble situation. They agreed to Christian mediation. They further agreed in writing that the decision by the arbitrators would be binding.

Each man chose one man — who was acceptable to both sides

125

— to sit on the "jury." The jury then chose a third man, a Christian specialist in building contracts. Both sides presented evidence. The jury handed down a compromise solution; the relationship had been restored.

In one year in Albuquerque, New Mexico, the Christian Conciliation Service — a division of the Christian Legal Society — arbitrated more than four hundred such disputes between Christians. The only cost was a fifty-dollar expense fee to the Christian lawyers who set up the procedure. No cases made the newspaper, and in many cases — including a number of divorce cases between spouses — the parties were reconciled.

This is perfect Scripture at work in an imperfect society. It proves to the world that we, as Christians, can solve our own problems.

If my older son disagrees with my younger son, I don't take them down to the courthouse and make them put up bail money. Nor do I have the sheriff serve them with a summons. Instead we have "court" around our dinner table. I'm the judge; the other children are the witnesses; my wife is the bailiff. So far we've settled every disagreement without paying legal fees.

That's because we are a family.

Only if a person proves himself to be a non-Christian (and refuses Christian mediation) am I free to consider the secular court. If he's a member of the family, however, we'll settle it "in house."

The church is moving rapidly into another age of persecution. Christians must be careful they are not numbered among the persecutors.

The bumper sticker sums it up: "Christians aren't perfect — just forgiven."

Now, if only we can learn to forgive one another — as God has forgiven us.

Thirty-eight

FACING THE
SANHEDRIN

DESPITE ALL God has done to break them up, sanhedrins, those religious courts charged with defending the faith, continue among us. In New Testament times the Sanhedrin, a council of seventy scholars with the high priest as chairman, was the supreme Jewish court of justice. Its task: to preserve the purity of the law.

The latest sanhedrin report comes from North Carolina, where the missions committee of a large church voted to withdraw financial support from one of their missionaries because he believes the gift of tongues is for today. The young missionary, whose name I cannot use because he is working in a highly sensitive African nation, was dismissed because the church's constitution "forbids giving financial support to missionaries not in accord with the church's doctrinal position."

In this case the church does not have an official doctrine. What it has is a tract ("printed and distributed by the hundreds") stating "the sign gifts have ceased and are not in the church today."

It also has a statement saying, "We believe the Bible disavows the authenticity of the sign gifts of prophecy, speaking in tongues, interpretation of tongues, miracles and healings for today and repudiates the experience-oriented theology and ecumenically oriented practice of the charismatic movement."

The church also is influenced by the statement of a Bible college which says, "Speaking in tongues is not for this age. The current charismatic involvement has its emphasis on experience and is in grave error."

These statements qualify as a modern Talmud which, when applied to a local congregation, are equivalent to the "halakah" (legal enactments) of present-day Jewry.

Last fall two deacons of the church accused the missionary of believing that the gifts of the Spirit are for this age. The missionary was home on furlough, and the week before he was to leave to return to the mission field he was brought before the committee for interrogation — much as Stephen appeared before the Sanhedrin. He responded with a loving but firm statement: "I do not believe that the gift of tongues has ceased. I do not find any clear teaching in the Scripture that it was a gift just for the 'apostolic age'.... 1 Corinthians 14:5 teaches that the purpose of tongues is for the edification of the church. Therefore as long as the church exists, so will the gift of tongues...."

When grilled, the young missionary gave a simple scriptural defense of 1 Corinthians 12-14, saying, "I don't think we should pursue or elevate the gift and give it an undue importance. I know some who teach that everyone should speak in tongues. They teach that unless you speak in tongues you are not Spirit-filled. I don't believe this. Paul clearly indicates all do not have this gift in 1 Corinthians 12:30."

The church officials were not vindictive — just bound by their traditions. The issue was even more confused because the missionary does not personally speak in tongues. However, his statement before the committee was so eloquent it deserves reprinting.

"If I didn't believe in the deity of Christ, or the inspiration of the Scriptures, or some other essential doctrine of the Christian faith, this would be something else. In the light of eternity, how important is the issue of tongues? Is our unity found in tongues or in Christ? Isn't it possible to be one in the Spirit and disagree on tongues?

"Since we are imperfect, fallible human beings, none of us has all the truth. Good, godly men down through the ages have disagreed on non-essential issues and will continue to do so until the end of time. On the mission field I work with others who do not agree with me in this issue, but we don't let this divide us. Why does it have to at [home]?

"The most important issue in all this discussion is not our differences over tongues, but how we love, accept and support each other in spite of our differences. In a world that is torn apart by war, racism, mistrust and disunity, shouldn't we, the body of Christ, be an example of love and unity? What kind of example are we before men when we break unity for such minor issues?"

He closed his powerful statement with a disturbing question.

"God has convicted me that I have only been exercising one-third of the ministry that Jesus and His disciples did.... The disciples had a three-pronged ministry: (1) sharing the gospel; (2) healing the people; and (3) casting out demons. There is a need for this in the country where I serve. I will start practicing this. God has been leading me in this.... I don't think I have any special gift in any three of these areas, but I do feel I should follow the example of Jesus and do what He did. Can we ever go wrong by following the example of Jesus?"

Sanhedrins, of course, always stone those who follow Jesus.

Ironically, the committee loved the missionary and respected his work. In a strange twist, while ruling that his "missionary commission by the church be rescinded and that his official church financial support be discontinued," they then became "talmudic" (trying to circumvent the law) by encouraging the church to give designated offerings to help with his support.

The missionary had asked: "Can we ever go wrong by following the example of Jesus?"

But Jesus said, "These things have I spoken unto you, that ye should not be offended. They shall put you out of the synagogues: yea, the time cometh, that whosoever killeth you will think that he doeth God service" (John 16:1-2, KJV).

The answer: You'll never go wrong by following the example of Jesus — but if you follow it closely enough, you too will wind up on a cross. Nailed there by your religious companions.

Thirty-nine

STICKS, STONES, CHRISTIAN BONES

SOMEONE ONCE said that everywhere the apostle Paul went they had a riot or a revival. Now all we can do is serve tea and cookies.

Not quite.

Riots are still much in vogue. But instead of non-Christians trying to kill Christians, it is now believers throwing stones at each other.

Every day, it seems, you can find a news article about a church split, scandal or lawsuit. Of course, we never read about those horrible blood-lettings in the Christian press. We're busy defending the kingdom. Rather, the articles appear in the secular press. And for every fight that makes the newspapers, there are hundreds of others which remain successfully hidden. These are the private wars accomplished by smiling hoodlums under the guise of love and honor.

More and more, however, God seems to be allowing those things formerly done behind the closed doors of church business meetings to become public.

It used to be a pastor could leave his wife and abscond with some sweet young thing half his age; a deacon could slug it out with a fellow deacon in the choir room over who gets to say the prayer at the Lord's supper; or the youth director could be fired because his wife wore slacks to the church picnic — and no one outside the chosen few would ever know.

Not so anymore.

Now, thanks to the miracle of the media, let a church treasurer be accused of stealing, let the head of a parachurch ministry use donations to buy a speedboat, and the entire world reads about it in the papers the next morning.

Take the case of a church in New Jersey — a tiny group of people who forgot to be good neighbors.

In a business meeting, thirty-seven of the church's sixty-two members met and voted to oust the pastor, who along with his family had founded the church ten years before.

The pastor, in turn, sued fourteen of the church leaders — including his father, two brothers, his sister, his aunt and uncle and two cousins. He claimed the vote was illegal. Besides, when he and his family founded the church, he was made "pastor-for-life" according to the church bylaws.

The whole mess wound up in Superior Court in Newark. I read about it in an English-language paper in Singapore.

The point is not whether church members will ever stop fighting. I predict churches will continue to battle each other, denominations will continue to split, and Christians will continue to bloody each other with stones as long as churches remain (a) social clubs rather than the "called out ones," (b) family fiefdoms rather than the body of Christ, (c) exclusive racial and cultural cliques rather than the koinonia, (d) a mixture of sprinkled (or dunked) heathens playing power games rather than the blood-washed saints who have relinquished all rights under the lordship of Jesus Christ.

Rather, the issue is how much longer God will allow our stupid, silly fightings to go undetected by others in the kingdom and hidden from the world at large.

Several years ago, when a deacon in a huge church in a large Southern city tried to wrest the microphone from the pastor and in a rage slugged him in the jaw in front of the entire congregation, very few of that denomination, and almost no one in the world, learned of the altercation. It was quickly hushed up on all counts.

After all, Christians reasoned, why air our dirty linen in front

131

of the public? If there is trouble in Camelot, who'll want to join our club?

Today, however, such an incident would make the headlines — probably with on-the-spot TV interviews with the red-faced deacon, the distraught pastor's wife, a local psychologist and a theologian from Princeton Seminary.

That may be healthy. In fact, it may be one of the things that will cause us to start acting like we preach.

Down here in Florida we have what is called the sunshine law. All government business must be conducted in the sunshine — in the open. No behind-closed-doors meetings are allowed.

Perhaps when Jesus said, "There is nothing covered that shall not be revealed," He was referring to church business meetings. When the lights go on in church closets, it means we will have to deal with the skeletons.

A few years ago one of the elders in a Florida church was indicted for selling unregistered securities and wasting money invested by some of the church members in his personal ministry.

The morning after the indictment the newspapers carried front-page headlines: CHURCH ELDER BILKS CHRISTIANS.

While some of the people were going about saying "tch-tch," the pastor was calling the newspaper and inviting them to send a reporter to the church the next Sunday morning.

"It's time the news media find out how problems should be handled in the family of God," he said.

The reporter didn't show up. But he did go by the church office on Monday and listen to the tape of the service, which contained the pastor's full explanation to the congregation, the tearful apology of the accused elder and the spoken statements of forgiveness on the part of some who lost money.

"I've been going after the wrong story," the reporter said after hearing the tape. "I thought Christians were like everyone else. But it's really news when you find people who forgive rather than fight."

We'll always have church problems. But when they are handled the way Jesus taught, the church will once again become a witness — not a scandal.

Forty

PHONY CHRISTIANS

A SIDE FROM disobeying and failing God, the one thing I fear most is becoming phony.

Our American world, in particular, has spawned far too many phony Christians. They are easy to spot, especially when it comes to money.

It's hard to tell, anymore, what a man means when he says, "Pray for me. I have a financial need."

Does he really want my prayers? Or my money?

As the overseer of a flock I struggle with this all the time. I am convinced God does not want church leaders begging for money. Nor does He want us to write letters to our mailing lists asking widows, struggling young couples and naive young Christians to "pray that God will meet our financial needs by next Tuesday." That is nothing more than manipulative begging.

Especially if you enclose an offering envelope.

I can't do much about the garbage which comes through the TV tube in the name of Jesus. Nor have I been very effective in stemming the tide of mail which comes from Bible-waving, Mercedes-driving beggars. But I can make certain that the leadership in our local body does not manipulate.

The danger, however, is not so much that our people might

misunderstand the genuine Christian's request for prayer. The real danger is that we, in our effort to keep the ministry pure, might stop asking our friends to pray for us.

Some of my "faith friends" love to talk about George Müller, who supposedly made his requests known only to God. Müller, though, never hesitated in letting everyone know exactly what his needs were. But that's different from today's phony Christian who says he wants to get you on his mailing list so he can "pray for you" (when what he actually wants is your money).

Although I know it is God who answers our prayers, I also know that money does not float down from heaven like manna. It is given by people who have received information about specific needs.

The danger lies in taking the shortcut — bypassing God and going directly to the people. The moment I do that I am looking to people as my source, rather than God.

My friend, the late George Sowerby, pastored a small charismatic church in Ft. Pierce, Florida. During the last years of his life George lived entirely by faith. He accepted no salary from his church.

He simply trusted God to speak to the right people, who in turn would meet his particular needs.

On occasion George would drive up the coast to ask me to join with him in prayer concerning some critical financial need. George never had a hidden agenda. When he asked for prayer, that's *all* he wanted. In these cases he always prefaced his request by saying, "If I share my need with you, it disqualifies you from meeting that need. *All* you are allowed to do is pray with me. You cannot give to me."

I respected George's commitment to this way of life. It was so different from the phony Christians who fill the airwaves and postal system with their veiled solicitations for money in the form of prayer requests. But I always felt frustrated. What if the Lord wanted me to be an answer to George's needs? My hands were tied, and I could not give — even if God told me to.

No, there is a better way. I prefer the way of my friends with Wycliffe Bible Translators. They use a slogan: "Full information. No solicitation." Or, as one of my wise old seminary professors used to say, "Trust God and tell the people."

Those of us in public ministry — in fact, all Christians — need the prayers of other Christians. And we need to be free enough to say "pray for us" and mean nothing more. We want to live pure in a dirty world. We want our motives to be noble. I hope I never deteriorate to the place where I start to bilk rather than trust.

I think about this each quarter when I write a thank-you letter that is included in the financial statements mailed to those who contribute through our church in Florida. How easy it would be to use double-talk. How easy it would be to say "thank you" while thinking, If I thank my friend for giving, he will give more.

How close I am each quarter to manipulating — using the gimmicks perfected by the mail-order and TV preachers.

Yet, as in requesting prayer for genuine needs, if I fail to say "thank you" for fear people will misunderstand, then we all lose.

It's easy to lock in on the high-profile phonies — and grow cynical. But in our judgment we must never forget the countless numbers of sweet, simple Christians who have not bowed their knee to Baal, who have no hidden agenda, no ulterior motives, who mean what they say when they say, "Pray for me." These are the ones whose yea is yea. God, give us more of them.

Part Seven

———

ON HOLIDAYS —
REALLY HOLY DAYS

Forty-one

To Whom Does Christmas Belong?

I S GOD'S grace just for Christians?

We Christians have a way of acting, well, exclusive, when it comes to our holidays.

Maybe it's because there are so few sacred seasons left anymore. First it was Halloween, once celebrated as the sacred eve of All Saints' Day, now a time of witches and demons.

Then it was St. Patrick's Day, which quickly deteriorated to the wearing-of-the-green and good luck in four-leaf clovers.

St. Valentine's Day followed suit, moving from a time of sacred celebration to candy boxes and sweetheart cards.

Thanksgiving, once a unique American holiday when the entire nation came together to worship God and give thanks, is now dominated by football, turkeys and more football.

Even Easter has gone secular, with more emphasis on rabbits than the resurrection.

The Jews, it seems, have been able to hold on to their sacred times much better than we Christians. Yom Kippur, Purim and the Passover remain times of sacred meaning. Hanukkah, the festival of lights, lingers in all Jewish minds as a great memory of a great people who overcame even greater hardships.

But Christians have let their religious holidays slip into the realm of the secular until much of the meaning is lost in busy commercial endeavors.

Thus, when Christmas rolls around, and it seems everyone from Minnie Pearl to Bloomberg's Department Store wants in on the act, well, maybe you can understand why Christians get a little puffed up.

After all, this is *their* holiday. Christ is the heart of Christmas. What right do others — Jews, Arabs and people who never go to church — have to get in on the act?

It does seem a bit strange, sometimes. My friend Ike Kornblat, who owns a department store and never, never goes to church (in fact, he never even goes to his synagogue), called me over to his cash register last Christmas Eve when I was making some last-minute purchases. Rubbing his hands as he punched the keys on his ancient register, he chuckled, "Do you know what my favorite song is in December? It's 'What a Friend We Have in Jesus.' "

I laughed with him, but someone standing nearby was offended. When we got out on the sidewalk, this person made it very plain that even though he shopped at Kornblat's Discount Store, he didn't appreciate the way this Jewish merchant took advantage of our "Christian holiday."

I remember several years ago when country singer Judy Collins picked up an old Christian hymn, "Amazing Grace," and turned it into the number-one hit song in the nation.

At that time there was a lot of self-righteous grumbling from Christians who seemed horrified that "Amazing Grace" was being sung in honky-tonks by singers high on drugs, or sandwiched between rock 'n' roll songs on a Top-40 radio station.

Yet isn't God's grace for all? If the good news of salvation were limited to churches, not very many people would have a chance.

In the final say, then, to whom does Christmas belong?

Last Christmas Eve Jackie and I were standing in our front yard. A group of carolers from the church had just pulled out, and we were standing in the darkness, thinking how fortunate we were to live in a nation where Christmas caroling was allowed.

Softly, we heard the strains of "Joy to the World" wafting through the woods next to our house. At first I thought the carolers had stopped on the road and were singing again. Then I realized the music was coming from our next-door neighbors' place.

We live in the country. Next door to our property is a retreat center for a Hindu group known as Yoga Shakti. They are mostly young people who have worked hard and built a small chapel which is surrounded by several acres of garden. Several times a year Yogas from all over the region gather to listen to their guru, a Hindu woman who comes from India to teach. Christmas is one of those occasions.

That night the Yogas, dressed in orange saris, playing wooden flutes and banging cymbals and tambourines, were dancing around in a circle in front of their little chapel singing:

> Joy to the world, the Lord has come
> Let earth receive her king.

I was offended. They had taken one of "our" songs and were singing it as though it belonged to them.

But to whom does Christmas belong?

To the Christian?

Should manger scenes be limited to church lobbies, or are they welcome in Jewish shop windows, the bars at motels and in the foyer at Macy's?

Should Christmas carols be sung only by choirboys, or is "Silent Night" appropriate in nightclubs as well — even when sung by those half drunk? And is the good news — the "joy to the world" — also for the Yogas?

Was it not to Jewish shepherds the first angels appeared? Did they not proclaim, "For unto YOU a child is born..."? So maybe Christmas really belongs to the Jews.

Was it not Arab wise men who came from far off Iraq and Iran, bringing gifts to the Christ child? Perhaps, then, Christmas belongs to the Arabs?

And what about those Yogas?

Like God's grace, Christmas belongs to all mankind. Let all the voices sing. Let all the merry bells ring out. Let joy flow like wine, and let all the people — those who say "Shalom," those who say "Salaam" and those who simply smile, wave flowers and say, "Peace, brother" — raise their glasses (or tambourines) in a common toast to God.

> Christ is born.
> Hallelujah!

Forty-two

A CHRISTMAS GIFT FOR DADDY B

M Y FATHER, whom we all called Daddy B, spent the first sixty-one years of his life accumulating things.
He moved to Vero Beach, Florida, in early 1919 and entered the citrus fruit business. A frugal man, he never went into debt. To my knowledge, he never owed a mortgage all his life.

As a result, by the time he was sixty-one he had accumulated a lot of things — real estate, citrus groves, businesses, houses and all the things you put in houses. Although he would not have been classified as wealthy, he never lacked for anything.

At age sixty-one he had a personal encounter with Christ. For the next twenty-six years, until he died in 1979 at the age of eighty-seven, he spent his life getting rid of the things he had accumulated.

He became the most giving man I have ever known.

My mother, who had her encounter with Christ about the same time, was the same way.

In fact, before my father died he appointed my older brother to oversee my mother's finances after he was gone. "If someone doesn't watch her," he chuckled, "she'll give away everything she has."

It was true.

My father, in particular, seemed bent on divesting himself of everything he didn't actually need prior to his homegoing. The only things he held on to were the things he wanted my mother to have after he left — things he felt necessary to her happiness.

Aside from that, he gave away everything else, including the old homestead of more than forty acres, which went to the Florida Baptist Convention as their retirement center. He gave a few personal things to his children and earmarked everything that did not go to my mother in his will for mission causes.

By the Christmas before he died, he and Mother had pretty well stripped themselves and their little house of all nonessentials. Daddy wanted to go to heaven the same way he came into this world — with empty hands. His treasure was, in fact, where his heart was.

The week before Christmas Jackie and I called our children together. We had a problem. What could we give Mother B and Daddy B for Christmas?

Two years before I had given them a full set of all my books — hardbound collectors' copies. They had read them and then given them away. "No need for books to sit here on my shelf when they could be out helping someone else," my daddy reasoned.

The year before I had given them an oil painting I had brought with me from the Philippines. It was a beautiful harvester scene in a mahogany frame. It never even made it to my parents' wall. They looked at it, said it was pretty and gave it away to someone who didn't have an oil painting.

Now our family was faced with a problem. What could we give my parents that they wouldn't give away?

I drove down to Vero Beach — forty miles south of our home on the east coast of Florida — on a reconnoitering mission. Maybe I could discover something they needed, something they wanted, which we could give them. Something they wouldn't give away.

My father was in bed the morning I arrived. His muscles had deteriorated badly, and although his mind was clear and sharp, he could no longer walk — or even sit up by himself. His arms worked fine, but the muscles in his back and the lower part of his body were weak and rubbery. Twice a day a friend came by to lift him into his wheelchair so he could sit at his desk and work on his ledgers.

I sat down on the side of the bed, and we talked for a while.

141

Then I asked him, point-blank, what he owned.

He grinned, waved his arm around the room and said: "You can see it all from where you are sitting."

He owned two pairs of soft khaki trousers, three shirts, one black bow tie, some underwear and a few pairs of socks — including some big white fuzzies to keep his feet warm. On his little nightstand were his hairbrush, his glasses, a pocket watch and a small radio. He owned no shoes, needing only an old pair of slippers for his wheelchair.

His long, narrow, single-bladed mother-of-pearl pocket knife, the one he used to slice grapefruit in the groves to test for sweetness, had been given to my brother.

Even his house had been sold to one of the children. As his outlook became more heavenly, his need for things diminished.

"What do you need?" I asked.

"I have everything I need," he smiled. "And," he added with a wink, "everything I want." He knew why I was there.

On the way out I looked around the house. My dad was right. Anything I gave them would be superfluous — and sooner or later given away. I returned home and reported to the family.

"Then let's give them something money can't buy," my daughter Robin said.

"Yeah," one of the younger children chimed in. "Let's give them us. They can't give us away."

It was a grand idea. We spent the afternoon planning it.

Christmas Eve day we all got in the car to drive down the coast to Vero Beach. Jackie and I and the five children — three of whom were students at Oral Roberts University, two still in high school.

We arrived midafternoon wearing our best church clothes. (I had rejected the idea of our teenage son, Tim, that we tie big Christmas bows around our necks so the grandparents would know we were giving ourselves as Christmas presents.)

My mother met us at the door, and after the usual hugs and kisses we all trooped back to Daddy B's bedroom. He was lying on his back, his head slightly elevated with a pillow, dressed as usual in his khaki pants, long-sleeved khaki shirt and white fuzzy socks.

When he saw us come in wearing our church clothes, he grinned and reached over on the night stand for his little black clip-on bow tie. "A gentleman should be properly dressed at all times," he said as he clipped the tie in place. At eighty-seven years of age, he remained, as always, proper.

We all gathered around his bed. My mother, almost eighty years old and dressed in a blue cotton dress with white pinafore, stood at the foot looking on. I announced we had brought our Christmas present — one they could not give away.

"We've come to give you ourselves," daughter Bonnie said.

Sandy had her autoharp. She strummed a chord, and we began to sing. We sang all the old Christmas carols. Mother B joined in with her faltering alto; Daddy added his bass. Then we told them we wanted to sing some of the Scripture choruses we sang at our church. They quickly learned them with us and joined in.

Then Mother B started a song. The kids grew silent as she sang from her Kentucky childhood.

> There's a church in the valley by the wildwood,
> No lovelier place in the dale.
> No spot is so dear to my childhood,
> As the little brown church in the vale.

Daddy B, Jackie and I joined her on the chorus; our children had grown up in a generation that missed that old gospel song.

> O come, come, come, come, come to the church in the
> wildwood....

There were tears in my father's eyes when we left. "I didn't tell you all the truth the other day," he said. "I said I had all I wanted, but I didn't. I wanted this. Like Mary, I shall keep it, ponder it in my heart and never give it away."

On the way back up the coast, heading for the Christmas Eve service at our church, our oldest son, Bruce, concluded the matter.

"I feel real clean," he said. "Like something holy has passed through me to Mother B and Daddy B."

Isn't that what happened that first Christmas — on that holiest of nights? God gave us something holy — something we can't give away.

Jesus can be shared. But once received, He never leaves us or forsakes us. He is with us forever.

What a grand gift!

Forty-three

CHRISTMAS:
A TIME
FOR WISHING

I SAT silently across the room, watching my three-year-old granddaughter turning the pages of the J. C. Penney Christmas catalog. Unaware of my presence, she was softly whispering the names of the hundreds of marvelous items pictured in the big "wish book" which lay across her knees.

"Fuzzy bear, rocky horse, bubble gum machine, roller skates, fire truck...."

I was mesmerized. Kristin's bright blue eyes twinkled as she put her stubby little finger on each picture.

"Cinderella doll, red wagon, Big Bird, tricycle...."

I listened carefully. Is it so wrong to wish?

I'm not sure I ever really believed in Santa Claus. But it was fun to wonder. And to wish.

Each year, early on Christmas Eve, Daddy would take us downtown. The main street, which was only three blocks long, ended at the park.

Pretty soon the city fire truck, siren howling, would arrive as the climax to the Christmas parade. Mr. O'Malley, who owned the restaurant, always dressed up like Santa and rode on the back of the truck. He carried a big bagful of hard candy and Cracker Jack boxes.

Each kid, no matter how poor, got something.

Then Mr. McWilliams, the mayor, would turn on the lights on the big tree in the center of the park next to the old World War I cannons. The choir from the Baptist church would sing carols, and the adults would join in — while the kids would go over to the cage where the big alligators snoozed in the water. We'd toss hard candy at them, hoping they'd snarl and snatch it up in their huge jaws. They never did. The candy would just bounce off their long noses and sink into the murky water. It was OK. Mother wouldn't let us eat the candy anyway.

Then it would be time to go back to the house. To wait. To wish. Is it so wrong to wish?

Christmas Eve was a time of wonderful expectation. Daddy would bring us together around the tree, which always stood in the same place, in a small alcove next to the stairs. The rest of the year an ancient spinning wheel sat there, but we kids knew that it was just guarding the spot until next Christmas when the tree would appear — that wonderful tree with the wonderful ornaments. When all the kids were in place, sitting cross-legged on the floor, Daddy would recite from memory:

'Twas the night before Christmas
And all through the house....

Lying in my bed upstairs, listening, I could hear the sound of my younger brother's breathing as he lay in the bed across the room. We would not speak. To do so would have broken the spell. But I knew he was wishing — as I was.

I wondered what it would be like, spending Christmas as my mother and daddy used to spend theirs — with snow on the ground and the sound of sleigh bells ringing...are you listening?... Instead there was the sound of the balmy Florida breeze rustling the leaves in the palm trees outside my window. Deep in the woods, beyond the orange trees, a pair of hoot owls would echo across the night. Sometimes, when the wind would die, you could hear the low roar of the ocean surf more than a mile away.

Would he come tonight? Would Donner and Blitzen find our house in the orange grove? Was Santa Claus really coming to town? If so, would he really show up in our fireplace where the stockings were hung by the chimney with care?

I'm grateful for that happy home of childhood, for it has left me with a life now filled with wonderful memories. I'm grateful for the sense of Christmas expectancy that I've brought with me into adulthood.

Life has a way, as you move into middle age, of becoming routine. The fascinations which once excited me are now slightly frayed; the things which once thrilled are sometimes tepid.

But once a year time turns backward in its flight, and on Christmas Eve I'm a child again — just for the night. Is it wrong to wish — as a child?

Where else does prayer begin — and faith start?

Long before I knew God, I would kneel beside my window.

> Star light, star bright,
> First star I've seen tonight,
> I wish I may, I wish I might,
> Have the wish I wish tonight.

C'mon! I know it's not a prayer. But it was the best I could do as a child. It wasn't until many years later, after Daddy became a Christian, that we started reading Luke 2 rather than " 'Twas the Night Before Christmas" on Christmas Eve.

But were all those other things wrong? Does not God sometimes use fantasy to prepare our hearts for reality?

The people I pity this Christmas are those who have no expectations. Those who no longer wish. The spiritual fuddy-duddies who have lost the wonder of childhood.

How easy it is to become sophisticated. Super-spiritual. To condemn Christmas trees and Santa Claus and the wonder of childlike wishing — because we've grown old...and correct.

"Cabbage Patch doll, red rabbit, toy piano, Jesus...." She looked up and saw me across the room. "Look, Pa-pa. Here's Baby Jesus in the manger. I wish for Him most of all."

I held her close so she could not see what was happening in my eyes.

I know there's a difference between wishing and praying, but for some of us it's the only way we can begin.

I hope I never grow so old, so stodgy, so theologically stiff that I no longer go to bed on Christmas Eve without listening for the sound of hoofbeats on the roof.

Forty-four

HEALING
THE HURTS
OF LIFE

I N HIS book *Some Things I Have Learned Since I Knew It All*, Jerry Cook tells the story of his open-heart surgery.

When he had his heart attack, Jerry was pastor of a large church in Oregon that believed in and practiced healing. During his recovery a woman in his church asked him, "Were you embarrassed to have a heart attack?"

Jerry replied that he was not embarrassed. But the woman was. She was unable to handle the totality of life's experiences — including the fact that pain and suffering are real.

Later, after he recovered, Jerry had a visit from a man who was fearfully facing the prospect of his own bypass surgery. "I want to see your scars," the man said shyly.

Jerry took off his shirt. The man gently traced with his finger the violet scar that ran vertically down Jerry's chest.

The man went on, "The doctor says the most painful part of the operation will be the surgery on my legs. They're going to take out veins from my calf to use in the heart bypass." Looking up at Jerry, he asked, "Can I see your legs?"

Jerry rolled up his pants. The man got on his knees. Without shame, he put his hands on Jerry's legs, touching the scars with his finger. When he rose to his feet, there were tears in his eyes.

"Thank you. Now I have hope."

Seeing and touching the scars gave him hope for survival.

Easter night Jesus appeared to His disciples. They were frightened and thought He was a ghost.

"Look at my hands and my feet," He said. "Touch me and see" (Luke 24:39).

Thomas was not in the room that night. Later he wanted to see His scars. Again Jesus obliged: "Put your finger here; see my hands. Reach out your hand and put it into my side. Stop doubting and believe" (John 20:27).

Jesus understands our need to see, to touch the scars. Once we do we know we can survive.

Sometimes our lives get scarred. And sometimes we're embarrassed because of them.

We think our scars are ugly — evidence of imperfection. We go to great expense and trouble to hide them with clothes and cosmetics. Sometimes we have them surgically removed.

Scars, though, are not evidence of imperfection but evidence of healing. Scars glorify God, who has brought us through.

I remember the afternoon I stood in our kitchen listening to our pregnant and discouraged daughter talking to her mother. It was Sandy's first baby, and she was afraid. In high school she had been president of her class, homecoming queen, the belle of all the balls. Now she was married, and although still beautiful, her stomach was expanding far beyond what she thought possible.

"I'm afraid I'll just explode," she told her mother tearfully — reaching out to hold her huge, awkward tummy with both arms.

"No," Jackie said, "you won't explode. Your skin just stretches."

"Then I'll go through life with baggy skin," she wailed.

Jackie chuckled. "Everything — including your skin — returns to normal. But there may be scars."

I stood to one side listening to this remarkable conversation. Marveling in the miracle of pregnancy and birth. Marveling even more in Jackie's ability to put her baby daughter's fears to rest.

Then Jackie did something absolutely wonderful. Standing there in the kitchen, she showed Sandy her waist and her abdomen. After five children, she's scarred.

"Stretch marks," she smiled, running her fingers along the ridges. "I call them love marks."

Reaching out her hand toward Sandy, she said tenderly, "Touch them."

Hesitantly, Sandy reached out her hand. Gently she let her fingers trace the scars.

"They look funny," Jackie said. "But every time I see them I think of you — and Bonnie and Tim and Robin and Bruce. Pregnancy has left me scarred. But my love for you makes it all worthwhile."

When I think of Mother's Day, I think of Jackie's scars.

Most Christians are scarred. We're not proud of them, but we're not ashamed either. When you're hurt, I pray God will send someone who will take your finger and let you trace their scars. Then after *your* scars are healed — and praise God they will heal — do the same for someone else. Scars are not ugly — they are evidence of God's healing.

Forty-five

GIVING
THANKS

ONE THING a man doesn't need when he's down is more condemnation.

A former pastor, a good friend of mine, had made some horrible mistakes last year. He got involved with a woman in his congregation. The church officials, without a blink, fired him — even though he had voluntarily broken off the adulterous relationship before confessing to his elders. Now he's struggling, not only because he's been denied the high honor of preaching, but because he's having to work at a secular job in the same town where he was disgraced. He told me how much it meant, when everyone else was running him down, to have one person call and say, "Thanks for what you meant to me and my family when we were going through a tough time."

My father died at the age of eighty-seven. On his eighty-first birthday I drove down the Florida coast to his home to spend part of the day with him.

"If you had to list the ten most significant things that have happened to you during your eightieth year, what would they be?" I asked.

He smiled and said, "I'd have to think about the last nine. But I can show you number one."

He got up from his chair at his desk and walked over to his filing cabinet. Sorting through the top drawer, he pulled out a letter and returned to his desk. It was from the chairman of the department of English literature in a large Midwestern university.

He read it to me as if he were reading from the Bible. "Sixty years ago," the professor said, "I sat in your high school English class at Delphi, Indiana. Rudyard Kipling, John Greenleaf Whittier, Henry Wadsworth Longfellow — they all came alive to me through your teaching. I went on to get my doctorate and eventually became chairman of the department of English literature at this university. Now I am retiring. I've thought of you many times but have never written. Today I write to say 'thank you.' "

My daddy lowered the letter. Tears glistened in his eyes and ran down his cheeks. "This," he said, smiling through his tears, "is the finest thing to happen to me this last year."

Thankful people smile. Self-righteous people sneer. Selfish people scowl. Recently, while walking through the supermarket, I passed a man wheeling a big cart of groceries. He looked at me and smiled. Even though I was scowling at the time (I always scowl in grocery stores), I found myself smiling back. Suddenly I felt good — and I smiled at the next person who passed. She, startled, smiled back. If we keep this up, I thought, the whole store will be smiling.

That's the way it is with saying "thank you." It's not enough to feel it. You need to express it. With a letter, a phone call or in person. And in the process you become a little more like Jesus.

Forty-six

HOPE FOR US ALL

M Y DADDY died in 1978. It was Sunday noon. We had just come in from church, and the phone was ringing. It was my mother in Vero Beach, Florida.

"Daddy has just gone to be with the Lord."

As long as I can remember she had called him Daddy. The kids all called him Daddy. Only his old friends — and he had outlived most of them — called him Walter.

Jackie and I went back out the door for the thirty-mile drive down the Florida coast toward the old home place. My mind was whirling. He was eighty-seven years old. Although his mind had been as sharp as when he taught English literature at DePauw University in 1915, we all had known the time was short.

Twenty-five years earlier, kneeling in his orange grove, his life goals had radically changed — from making money to giving it away. Now he was satisfied. He owned nothing. He was ready to go home.

The week before, I had sat on the side of his bed, listening as he quoted from Longfellow:

Tell me not, in mournful numbers,
Life is but an empty dream! —

For the soul is dead that slumbers,
And things are not what they seem.

I knew, in his poetic way, he was telling me he was about to die. It didn't seem to bother him. He believed death was a beginning — not an end.

I believed that too. At least I wanted to. But as I drove along in silence, Job's question kept swirling through my mind: "If a man dies, will he live again?" It's the question we all ask when death strikes.

"Daddy has gone to be with the Lord," my mother had said. How did she know? How does anyone know where you go when you die? What's to prove we're not like ants stepped on by kids, or like leaves burned in the fireplace?

We pulled up in the carport and went inside. Mother met us in the kitchen. "He went peacefully, in his sleep. I've already had my cry. He's back there on the bed."

"I'll call the funeral director," Jackie said softly. "You go on back."

I entered the familiar room. Daddy's body was on the bed, the tan blanket pulled up over his chest. His mouth was partially open, his arm hanging at an awkward angle off his bed. Looking down at him, I could almost hear Longfellow again, echoing in the empty room:

Life is real! Life is earnest!
And the grave is not its goal;
Dust thou art, to dust returnest,
Was not spoken of the soul.

I knelt beside his bed. His body was still warm, but his arm had already grown stiff. I bent it back under the covers, caressing his hand as I did so. For the first time I cried. Jackie came into the room, her hand on my shoulder as I wept.

I finally stood, my arm around her waist, looking out the window at the Florida he loved so much. "Eternal springtime," Daddy used to call it, reminding us of the harsh winters back in Indiana.

"He's still here, isn't he?" Jackie said.

"I feel him too. He hasn't left yet."

153

Then, in silent words, he spoke to me. I've examined that sacred moment many times since then. Was I imagining? Was I wanting to believe so desperately that I just made it up? No, for when I talked to my wife later, she had sensed virtually the same thing.

"You think Florida is beautiful? What you see out the window, son, is nothing compared to what I see."

My doubt was gone. In its place was hope. Not the kind of hope that says, "I hope he's alive." Rather it was the biblical kind: "We have this hope as an anchor for the soul, firm and secure" (Heb. 6:19).

All of that came to mind last night as I was driving home. I passed a blue dump truck with a picture on the door — an empty cross on a hill. Under it were three words: He is risen!

Hope. Even on the door of a dump truck.

Easter is God's message of hope to the people of this planet.

"If a man dies, will he live again?" wrote Hugo Gryn, a London rabbi, of his horrible experiences in a Nazi concentration camp.

Another Jew answered with more than words — He answered with His life.

"Why do you look for the living among the dead?" the angel asked at Jesus' tomb.

That day in 1978, as I held Daddy's lifeless hand, the angel whispered again. "He is not here. He is risen!"

Hope for all of us!

Forty-seven

MY FINEST
CHRISTMAS

I HAD known for several months that my body could not maintain the pace. The time was December 1979. The pressures in our church had brought us to another crisis stage.

Writing deadlines, to which I had agreed the year before when things were less hectic, were now screaming frantically at me from the finish line.

Then there was the traveling ministry. I enjoyed it because I could go into a different city each week and be treated like a king — and not have to live with or solve the problems I constantly created at home.

Running on wound-up energy, I was growing less and less effective in all I was doing.

I first realized I was in big trouble in early December when I stepped off a plane in Bogota, Colombia. After stumbling through customs and finding myself standing on a dark curbside outside the airport terminal, I suddenly realized I didn't know where I was staying or who was meeting me.

It was an empty feeling. I was surrounded by my suitcase and boxes of supplies I wanted to deliver to missionaries. I wanted to sit down on the curb and cry. What in the world was I doing here anyway? I wanted to be home.

Suddenly I heard a horn blowing. I looked up. There was an old friend — a native Colombian. He was motioning for me to get into his car. In a daze I did.

"What are you doing here?" I asked.

"I was praying, and the Lord said to go to the airport and meet Jamie."

"I don't understand."

"You had written earlier, saying you were coming and would stay with me. But you never said when. Each night I have prayed. Tonight the Lord said you had arrived and needed help."

I remember little about the trip to South America except the conversation I had with a friend on the plane back home. I was to arrive home in mid-December, then leave the day after Christmas for South Africa — returning home in mid-January via Israel. I said to my friend, "I don't see any way to slow down except to be struck down."

"Don't curse yourself with that," he said.

"It would be a blessing, not a curse," I mumbled.

Christmas fell on Tuesday that year. On the Thursday before, Jackie and I attended our home group meeting — a group of five couples out of our church who meet weekly.

During the week I had been home I had started getting criticized by some leaders inside our church over a written proposal I had made on future plans. They had been stung by my wording, drafted on the plane between Panama and Miami. None had come to me personally, but they were mouthing their anger to others. I heard about it, naturally, and was not handling it well. At the home group meeting I opened up and expressed my confusion and my inability to come up with the necessary wisdom to draw conclusions.

In short, I was weary.

That group prayed a dangerous prayer: "Lord, do whatever You have to do to get Jamie back in right relationship with You." I knew it was dangerous to pray that way, but I added an "Amen!" I was desperate.

That night when I got home my right lower leg was red and swollen. By bedtime I was feverish. Friday Jackie insisted I see a doctor. He glanced at it, gave me a shot of penicillin and said to come back next week. I was in bed all day Friday and Saturday with fever. Sunday morning I felt better but was woozy. Somehow I stumbled through the service.

Alice King was a medical doctor in our congregation. She grabbed me after the service and asked, "What's wrong?" When I told her, she sat me down on the front row of the auditorium, took off my shoe and sock, and pulled up my pants leg.

"You have a blood clot in your leg!" she said with alarm. "It's called phlebitis. Get in the back seat of my car and prop your leg up — now. I'm going to take you to your home, and you're going to bed — with your leg elevated higher than your body."

So with several of the men supporting me I hobbled out of the church, went home and got in bed — where I stayed for three weeks.

I discovered some things. When my wife called South Africa and said I was sick and couldn't come, the brothers accepted it. But I knew if she had called and said, "He's tired," or "He doesn't feel God wants him to come," they would have been upset.

The same was true with my publishers — who willingly pushed back the deadlines. Friends wanted to come and rebuke the devil. But it wasn't the devil who needed rebuking. It was me.

As a wonderful bonus I was able to spend Christmas at home, surrounded by the happy sounds of all my children. Even though I was upstairs in bed, I was alive. It was my finest Christmas, so far.

Part Eight

ON CHRISTIANS IN THE MARKETPLACE

Forty-eight

No More Schlock

THE OLD German *schlockmeister* had a stall in a back alley where he sold cheap, shoddy merchandise. Today *schlock* has become the byword for anything trashy.

In recent years the schlockmeister has started selling Christian merchandise. It started innocently with things like dove license tags. In fact, I still have mine on the front of my car.

Then things quickly got out of hand. Like the bumper stickers that read, "Honk if you love Jesus" or, "In case of rapture this car will self-destruct."

Expanding their trade, trash merchants joined the Christian Booksellers Association and set up booths at the annual conventions. Bookstore owners, seeing a way to stock low-ticket inventory that moved rapidly, began filling their shelves with Holy Hardware, known in the trade as Jesus Junk: luminous light switches that glowed in the dark with the message "Jesus is the light of the world"; scented "stick-ups" for the bathroom that read, "Jesus perfumes my life"; "Junkies for Jesus" T-shirts; "Hallelujah" rump patches for jeans.

The Christian marketplace began to take on the appearance of the outer court of the temple where merchants sold doves and lambs for sacrifice. It was there, you remember, that Jesus took a whip and, eyes blazing, drove the money-changers from the temple. "You've taken a house of prayer and turned it into a den of thieves," he shouted.

During the Dark Ages religious schlockmeisters sold relics and indulgences. Today they use direct mail and promise you a miracle if you send them money in return for some cheap gimmick.

Pictures of Jesus are plastered on everything from watches to T-shirts. He's not only upstaged Mickey Mouse, but He's also become the pawn of Christian hucksters who have substituted for the verse about "casting pearls before swine" the words of Phineas T. Barnum: "There's a sucker born every minute."

Schlock!

Last year while flipping through the pages of one of my favorite Christian magazines, I was jolted by a catalog insert advertising "Christian" clothing, promoted like the high-priced stuff from Banana Republic. There were Fruit of the Spirit shirts — far more spiritual than Fruit of the Loom — that came in plum, tangerine and raspberry. Women could order a shapely "Magdala" sweater — similar to that worn by Mary Magdalene. *Gasp!*

A reserved British friend who had seen the same ad wrote in justified protest: "It is enough to make one lose one's lunch."

We Americans are blind to how our cultural Christianity is viewed by the suffering church overseas. One Nepalese Christian, who had just been released from prison after three years of horrible torture for the crime of teaching a Bible class in his village, wasn't very impressed when he came to the States. Shortly after he arrived, a well-meaning schlockmeister gave him a "Jiving for Jesus" T-shirt with a picture of a Christian rock group on the back. When asked why he didn't wear it, he politely replied he couldn't wear short-sleeved shirts. He needed something to protect the still-tender scars on his arms where the prison guards had burned him with a red-hot poker.

I'll never forget the sad expression on his face as he sat in front of a TV set watching a certain American televangelist, wearing a sequined vest and weighted down with so much gold he would sink if tossed into a baptistry, talk about "taking up the cross."

Not all merchandising is religious garbage, of course. Works of art. Christian symbols. All have their place as long as they are in good taste. I thank God for those who create works of art for the glory of God — and for those who distribute them. We have a number of beautiful plaques on the walls of our home with Scripture messages on them. My wife sometimes wears a tiny gold dove around her neck. She purchases greeting cards and personal stationery with Christian symbols and Bible verses — all done in good taste. I have a small silver fish embossed on the front of my attaché case, hoping it will serve as a conversation starter on airplane trips. I am grateful for works of art — great and small.

But before buying such items I always ask myself one question: If Jesus were here today, would He buy this? Can you imagine our Lord riding a donkey into Jerusalem on Palm Sunday with a bumper sticker on its rump: "Bray if you love Jehovah?"

Shoddy junk, cheap merchandising, the inferior trash that floods the Christian marketplace in the name of our Lord and Savior should have no place in our lives. God is calling His children to holiness and excellence. That means, among other things, no more schlock.

Forty-nine

THE CHRISTIAN AND HIS MONEY

EVERY SERIOUS Christian I know struggles with the place of money. In fact, when I meet a Christian who does not struggle with it, I wonder just how serious he really is.

Jesus had more to say about money — and man's relationship to it — than any other subject. It's not wrong to make money. In fact, Paul says if a man doesn't work he shouldn't eat. But the more we earn, the harder it is to maintain a proper relationship with God. And if we ever become rich, Jesus said, there's a real danger we might not even make it to heaven.

The danger is real, you know. I know at least ten influential churches whose pastors began making big bucks. Then they got involved in scandals — either sexual or financial — and the churches lost their influence. Some of the pastors were able to stay at their churches, but ministry has become their number-two priority. Holding on to what they have is number one.

Too many of my friends have grown rich and slipped their spiritual moorings only to float away in their Mercedes — tragically powerless while justifying their wealth.

Remember Luther's supposed reply to the church official who bragged, "No longer does the church have to say, 'Silver and gold have I none....' "

"Yes," the reformer answered, "but neither can she say, 'In the name of Jesus rise and walk.' "

Not wanting this to happen, official church boards have been notorious in protecting their pastors and staff members from ever having to face the temptations of riches. "Lord, keep me poor and humble," the old pastor prayed in the deacons' meeting.

One of the deacons responded, "You keep him humble, Lord. We'll keep him poor."

But this stingy attitude totally overlooks what Paul says about God's men receiving "double honor." That means, I take it, the pastor should be paid twice as much as the chairman of the finance committee.

I grew up believing I should tithe. My wife and I tithed our first paycheck after we were married. I was earning $1.19 per hour as a city bus driver for the Ft. Worth Transit Company. Writing out a check for $4.76 each week to the University Baptist Church was a wonderful discipline. We gave and trusted God to supply all our needs. He's never failed us.

But there was little joy. God required me to "pay" my tithe every paycheck. I tithed because I had been taught that everything I had belonged to God.

What a miserable interpretation of New Testament stewardship. If my car belonged to God, why did it keep breaking down? If my house belonged to God, why did the toilet stop up? No, my house is mine. Not God's. My money is mine too. The question I'm faced with is even tougher though: What am I doing with my money — spending it on self or for His glory? Can a Christian, for instance, ever justify a huge diamond ring as long as others are starving?

When I first began writing, I wrote for the joy of it — and because I believed my books and articles would minister to those who read them. Fortunately, my books have sold, and I've made enough money to buy my house and put my children through college. Most important, we've been able to give away huge amounts. I praise God for that. In other words, it's OK to get in order to give.

Now I am struggling with how much money is enough. In the early days of my ministry I looked with disdain on those who ministered for money — who set a price tag on each sermon. Some celebrity Christians would not come to town for less than seven thousand dollars plus expenses. It's because of overhead, their agents justified. I determined not to judge — and never to do it that way myself.

But recently I've wondered. I have a big ministry project I want to see accomplished. I need money to do it. The only way to get it done — apart from begging — is to sell my services. Therein lies the struggle.

How should I respond when a sponsoring group asks, "How much do you charge to speak?" I have no problem negotiating a book contract. But preaching?

If Paul Harvey can command twenty-five thousand dollars for a single speaking engagement, why shouldn't a preacher set a fee? Does that make him a hireling?

One of the men in my home group reminds me there's nothing wrong with making money. He says he gets up every morning and goes to work to do just that. Yet when it comes to preaching, it's just possible that a different set of principles may apply.

In an editorial in *The Wittenburg Door*, Mike Yaconelli says, among other things, that Christians have justified making money by saying it is not money which is the root of all evil but the *love* of money.

"Radical faith doesn't mean that we all give up our money and become indigent, but it does mean that we give up the antiquated illusion that money isn't evil," Yaconelli says. "We must face up to the frightening fact that anything money touches, it corrupts — including us."

Is money really evil? I think not. Like power and sexual freedom, however, evil always lurks in its shadow. Few are able to resist it. Therefore a periodic money checkup is mandatory — not to see how much we have, but to see what it is doing to us.

The bottom line? I must make my decisions based on what God says. If money is a by-product, I shall rejoice. If it costs me something rather than pays me something, I shall rejoice also. Anything else means I am a materialist — and a man cannot serve God and mammon.

Fifty

ANATOMY OF
A DECISION

A LTHOUGH THE offer to write THE book on the PTL scandal had not been nailed down, it was there just the same.

In May the agents started calling. The dollars the publishers were willing to pay to get the inside story — if it had the right byline on it — were incredible.

The big money would come for the book and possibly a movie. During negotiations as much as $3 million in advance was proposed. My share could be as much as 40 percent.

I started spending the money — in my mind.

I am deeply committed to the task of Bible translation. Half the money, I dreamed, would be given to translate the Word for Bibleless people.

For years I've wanted an inside baptistry in our church, but we'd never had the money to install one.

I would love to set up some kind of savings account for my grandchildren.... My wife needs a new car.... The air conditioning on my pickup truck is broken...so is our dishwasher....

Yet inside something was wrong. Was it right, before God, to make money off someone else's sin?

Would my collaboration on a book project be viewed as an

endorsement of someone else's life-style?

Was I willing, for the sake of money, to follow the rich and famous with a broom and shovel?

More important, was I in danger of prostituting — selling my gift for money?

I had watched, with growing disgust, the public spectacle on TV. Why? Why do all these people want to come before the unbelieving public and say all these horrible things about one another, even if they are said with a smile and cached in the pious phrases of Zion? Do they do it to glorify God? To feed the sheep? To build the kingdom? To save the lost?

Then I looked at myself and saw that I was in the same boat as all the rest of the publicity seekers. Only I was not considering my face on "Nightline" or "Face the Nation" — I was considering my name on a book that would sell a million copies at $17.95 at a 15 percent royalty of which I might get half.

As a writer I had never worked as a prostitute, only as a lover. Both prostitute and lover offer the same product, but one does it for what he can get, the other does it for what he can give.

The first week of June I was to be in Israel for six days of research. I planned to go back to Israel in October to videotape a series of teachings on the miracles and parables of Jesus — filmed on the actual locations where they took place. A tour group would be accompanying me, traveling from site to site as my audience. Chuck Colson's organization, Prison Fellowship, would distribute the videos in the prisons of America. The purpose of my June trip was to visit all thirty sites — from Jerusalem to Galilee — where we would later set up our cameras.

My wife and friends wisely counseled me to put my decision about the book on hold until I returned from Israel.

The day before I left for Israel I was in a church staff meeting. As we served holy communion one of our staff pastors read from Jesus' words in John 5:30: "...I seek not to please myself but him who sent me."

How does one please God?

All the way to Israel I struggled with the entire process of making decisions. What, I asked myself, are the major factors in decision making in our Western culture? Our lives are filled with decisions: What job do I take? Where shall I live? Shall I buy or build? Where should I send my children to school? What about retirement? The criterion for each decision is always one thing: money.

Is that wrong? Are we not supposed to be good stewards? Is money evil, or just the love of money?

Then I was in Israel, walking the land, climbing the mountains. I stood where Abraham told Lot, "You take the green pastures of the Jordan Valley. I'll take the desert."

I stood in Wadi Kelt, where the ravens fed Elijah.

I contemplated Jesus' words to the rich young ruler about selling all.

I could not find a single Bible hero who made decisions based primarily on money. Those who did went down in infamy: Balaam, the rich young ruler, Judas, Ananias and Sapphira. I struggled with my own decision.

Would I write this book, I asked myself, if I only got a fair return, not a fortune?

Maybe I should put out a fleece as Gideon did. But fleeces are for cowards. Jesus told Peter His church would be built on those who received knowledge by revelation. It's OK to be directed by circumstances, but far better to hear God in your heart and act on it. Then, when you sleep, you sleep with a clear conscience.

I returned home Saturday night. Sunday morning in the pulpit I announced to my people that I cannot write primarily for money and cannot write someone else's book. They greeted my decision with sustained applause.

Battling jet lag, I went home at noon and went straight to bed. My oldest son, Bruce, who lives next door, came into the bedroom. "I'm proud of you, Dad. I know some of that money would have trickled down to us kids. But I learned something from you today — obeying God is more important than making money."

He squeezed my shoulder and closed the door gently. I closed my eyes and thought, That million dollars could not purchase what you just gave me, my son. I drifted off to sleep with a clear conscience.

Fifty-one

OWE
NO
MAN

I BOUGHT my first pair of shoes — I mean the first pair I bought by myself without my parents being there to approve — when I was thirteen years old.

I had walked into my dad's office in downtown Vero Beach, Florida. My dad was the silent partner in an insurance business, the Buckingham-Wheeler Insurance Agency. Mr. Wheeler had the front offices. My dad's offices were in the rear where he carried on his business as the executive secretary of a number of small corporations.

Daddy was always concerned about the way his boys looked. "You can tell a gentleman by looking at the heels of his shoes," he said. "Any bum can make the toes shine by wiping them on the back of the opposite leg of his trousers. But a gentleman's shoes are always shined on the heels as well as the toes."

Even today I find myself, when introduced to someone for the first time, glancing down to see if the heels of his shoes are shined.

That afternoon I had ridden my bike from the schoolhouse, only four blocks from the center of the little town, and stopped by my dad's office. When I walked in he was sitting at his big desk in the back of the insurance office. His adding machine was near his right hand; his big black ledger books with green pages, where he kept records of all the citrus fruit shipped from his packing house, were in front of him. He glanced down and said, "You need new shoes."

"Can't I wait until later? I'm supposed to meet some of the guys."

"Before Sunday," he said.

Friday afternoon after school I parked my bike in front of Wodtke's Department Store, right across the street from the Buckingham-Wheeler Agency, and went in to buy a pair of shoes — the first I'd ever bought on my own.

Mr. Wodtke himself waited on me. When you live in a town of three thousand, everybody knows everybody. It's a good, warm feeling. The Wodtkes were Catholic, but as far as I knew they didn't drink or anything. Besides, my dad never objected to doing business with good Catholics. It's just that we boys were always warned never to date Catholic girls. "You never can tell when you might fall in love. Then you'd have to sign a contract with the priest, be married in the Catholic church and raise your children as Catholics."

My friend Eddie Trent later married Kay Wodtke, who was in my class at school. I never did find out if he had to sign one of those contracts.

"I'm sure your dad will approve of these, Jamie," Mr. Wodtke said. "I'll send him a bill at the end of the month." They cost $4.50.

I walked my bike across the street, parked it in front of my dad's office and headed back to show him my shoes.

"Did you pay Mr. Wodtke?"

"No, sir, he said he'd send you a bill."

My dad got up from his chair, reached in his wallet and pulled out a five-dollar bill. "Buckinghams never go into debt," he said. "Go across the street and pay Mr. Wodtke now. And never go into debt again — for anything."

That lesson grows more and more important in my life as I look at what debt is doing to our nation, to young couples and others who didn't have a daddy like mine.

My dad felt debt had but one purpose — to be paid. Immediately!

Daddy was one of the few businessmen in our little town who

went through the Great Depression unscathed. That was because he "owed no man." It took him nineteen years to build his house after he was married. But when that magnificent sixteen-room, solid redwood house was finished, it was debt free.

Mortgage fell into the same category as adultery, playing cards and whiskey. In my own mind I somehow tied it in with a dreadful place called the poorhouse. I'd never seen a poorhouse. I'd never met anyone who had seen one. But the subject came up ever so often in our home, and it was associated with mortgage. If you had a mortgage, sooner or later you'd wind up in the poorhouse.

I've not stuck to the letter of his advice, but I do live by the spirit of his law. I use a credit card — but always pay it off at the end of the month. Besides that I live by a personal law: "Never buy anything on time that does not appreciate."

Most houses appreciate. So does land. Automobiles don't. Neither do TV sets, waterbeds or face lifts. One year when our church went through a friendly split and our income dropped 30 percent for eight months, I can't tell you how grateful I was we didn't have a mortgage. Had we been in debt, the only way we could have kept out of the poorhouse would have been to raise money the way some do, by selling charismatic indulgences — called premiums.

We live in a nation that does not take its debt seriously. Many Christians borrow money and never expect to pay it back. One banker told me he never loans money to preachers or people opening "Christian businesses." Personal bankruptcy is just as acceptable as abortion. Bankruptcy may be OK if the action is to buy you time so you can repay your bills. But who does? We just continue buying things we can't pay for, then get angry when the debtor demands his money.

Daddy was right. The only sure way to keep from becoming an alcoholic is never to take a drink. The only sure way to stay out of the poorhouse is to stay out of debt.

Fifty-two

WOULD JESUS DRIVE A MERCEDES?

CLARENCE JORDAN was the first and probably only man I've ever heard speak who, had he pointed his finger at me and said, "Lay down your nets and follow me," I would have followed.

Maybe that's because he was one of the few men I've ever met who knew exactly where he was going.

The year was 1953. I was a junior English major at Mercer University, a Baptist school in Macon, Georgia. Ray Brewster, who was the university chaplain, had invited Jordan (pronounced JUR-dan in south Georgia) to drive over from Koinonia Farms, the community near Americus that Jordan had birthed in the fifties, to speak to the Baptist ministerial students. Brewster made a special trip up to my room in the ATO fraternity suite to invite me.

Why me? I wasn't a ministerial student. I was cynical, active in campus politics and athletics, with no good word for the campus preacher-boys. Perhaps, as I think back to that time, Brewster sensed I was struggling with God's call on my life. I agreed to go hear this man who had given up his secure position as professor of Greek at Southern Baptist Seminary to start the South's first interracial farm.

Koinonia Farms was my first exposure to community. Clarence Jordan was my first exposure to someone who was willing to give his life to follow Jesus. Every other Christian I knew — including myself — used the teachings of Jesus to justify their worldly life-style. Jordan was determined to live the life-style of Jesus.

Only about five or six of the more than 150 ministerial students on campus turned out to hear him. After listening, I could understand why.

He was poor. I mean he was poor on purpose. His hair needed cutting. His suit (I discovered it was borrowed) was frayed and unpressed. He and the handful of others who lived in the simple buildings on the farm held all things in common. That was radical enough to cause the area residents to accuse him of being a communist. Not only that, blacks as well as whites were welcome at Koinonia Farms. That was radical enough — in the fifties — to cause the area residents to dynamite his buildings, fire shotguns at his old car as he drove down the road at night and burn crosses on the community's property.

He spoke that afternoon about how "the foxes have holes and the birds of the air have nests, but the Son of Man has no place to lay his head.... Follow me, and let the dead bury their dead." Few leap to their feet and say, "Send me!" after that kind of message. But my heart burned within, for I knew this man represented Jesus.

It was Clarence Jordan who asked that afternoon, "If Jesus were here today, would He drive a Mercedes?"

I am not one of those who believes that Jesus wants us all poor. Neither am I one who believes Jesus wants us all rich. Jesus wants us to have enough to do what He's called us to do.

A friend who works with Habitat for Humanity, an organization made up of people (former President Jimmy Carter is one of them) who donate their time to build houses for the poor, wrote to me recently. Tony Campolo had just spoken to their group and asked, "Is it a sin to own a BMW?" (That's a yuppie Mercedes.) Then he added, "If Jesus had forty thousand dollars, would He buy a BMW or use that to feed or house the needy in the Third World?"

People get dynamited for asking questions like that. Or crucified.

Tony, however, said one woman was so struck by one of his

talks that she wrote his ministry a check for the same amount that she paid for her custom drapes. It built three houses in Haiti.

The question, of course, is not about custom drapes or expensive automobiles. It is about attitude.

Recently I wrote my younger brother, John, who is in family medical practice in Birmingham, Alabama. I asked if he wanted to go with me to Israel. His reply devastated me: "I hope God will someday allow me to see the Jordan, walk to Calvary's mountain, sit on the hillside by the Sea of Galilee and walk on the Jericho road where the Good Samaritan showed the world what it meant to live the life of love. I just can't forget, however, my visits to the diseased Mayans in the poverty-stricken nation of Belize. If they had only one clinic, they would not be crippled, blind, or mentally incompetent. In a poor country, prevention is the only hope. I cannot go to Israel and build that clinic also."

Like Clarence Jordan, John had set his priorities.

Would Jesus drive a Mercedes? Oral Roberts, in a refreshingly candid revelation about his finances, says he drives a Mercedes.

But that's not the question. The question is: What does God want *me*, not Oral, to drive?

I never saw Clarence Jordan after that dreary winter afternoon in early 1953. He returned to Americus and lived out his life helping the poor. He worked side by side with his wife, Florence. People continued to try to kill him but never were quite successful. We never corresponded. I never visited Koinonia Farms, but I read everything I could find about it. For, you see, his question still haunts me.

What would Jesus drive?

Part Nine

———

ON LIVING *IN* THE WORLD, BUT NOT BEING *OF* THE WORLD

Fifty-three

THE RISK
FACTOR

DURING MY senior year in high school a group of women somewhere in the nation started a movement to have all competitive sports — especially football — removed from public schools. Team sports, they complained, were too traumatic. Children, they argued, should not be led to believe their team could win, then suffer the trauma of losing. They should only play games where everyone wins.

They did not stop to think that there can be no victory where there is no possibility of defeat.

Defeat is definitely traumatic. But so is childbirth. And graduation. And marriage. Yet all are part of life. To eliminate them simply because they are risky would mean the cessation of life.

The risk-free life is a victory-free life. It means lifelong surrender to the mediocre. And that is the worst of all defeats.

Today's youth are deathly afraid of risk. Yet, in what must be one of history's great ironies, desiring safety, they escape into drugs — which is guaranteed failure and death.

Political freedom demands risk. Eliminate the risks of freedom and you establish a slave state. Today's liberal is constantly crying for justice. But the question is not justice; it is freedom. Most definitions of justice call for the elimination of risk.

Capitalists love monopolies which eliminate risk. But in the process monopolies kill the wonderful creativity birthed — as with team sports — through competition.

Politicians work at gerrymandering to control their power positions in government — trying to eliminate the risks of defeat.

I asked a congressman friend of mine what was the first thing a president, senator or congressman thinks of after election. He smiled sadly, "How to be re-elected." Once in office the elected official spends all his time building a power base to protect his vested interests. If he can eliminate risk for us by providing us with all kinds of government benefits, we will keep him in office.

Those who have the most to lose, however, are those least prone to risks and to bold actions. Take the banks, for instance. Banks do not like risk-takers. In fact, they are constantly asking what the risk factor is in a loan. Therefore bankers invest in established success, which means that banks invest in the past — not the future. Visionaries don't have a chance.

I've seen the same thing with publishers. In the past I've tried to get established publishers to innovate in new concepts of communication, such as video materials, compact discs, radio and TV. I met with massive resistance.

The bold, enterprising and innovative work that went into the birth of computers came from young outsiders — not from those still working with pen and paper who lacked the ability to dream and the willingness to risk.

The major political and social impact of recent years came from student movements and minority uprisings — from those who had little to lose and hence were ready to lose it. Their causes meant more to them than the penalties they risked.

Jesus was such a Man. So were Martin Luther and John Wycliffe. Martin Luther King was such a man. So is Oral Roberts. All risk-takers, courting defeat while taking extraordinary risks.

To dream of a risk-free world is to imagine a creation without hell. But a creation without hell is also a creation without heaven. God has made us to be creatures who are forced to choose between good and evil — which is the greatest of all risks.

The only risk-free world is in the minds of evil or lazy men — for God is a God of great risk. He sent His Son. Even more, He's entrusted the church to us. Those who dream of a risk-free life are sooner or later all losers.

Fifty-four

"HERE COMES THE JUDGE"

S EVERAL YEARS ago the president of a national Christian
fund-raising organization was convicted, along with two
assistants, of *conspiring* to steal money from a widow.

The jury, swayed by a smooth-talking lawyer, granted more
than two hundred thousand dollars in damages to the plaintiff,
plus demanded repayment of the money she had lost.

The fund-raising organization was obviously wrong for taking
money it could not repay. But even the plaintiff was surprised at
the fierce way the judge and jury acted toward men who had
clearly made mistakes but were not, by any stretch of the imagi-
nation, guilty of intentionally conspiring to steal.

We are living in a world which is becoming more and more
hostile to the gospel message — and the gospel messenger. Even
the smallest mistakes are being blown out of proportion by the
enemies of the kingdom. Every means possible is being used to
discredit those who preach the gospel of Jesus Christ.

This nation has always been sympathetic to the gospel. However, many are predicting that by the end of the century America
will no longer be a haven for Christians or Christianity.

In many areas of the nation committed Christians are already
being counted as enemies of society — much as those early Chris-

tians were in Rome and the Middle East. Within a few years it will not only be acceptable to persecute Christians openly — it will be popular.

Cultural Christians will always be acceptable in this world. That is because they are like chameleons, able to adapt to the color of the foliage.

But the friendly environment of the past is changing rapidly. The wise Christian understands this — and watches his step. One false move will mean exposure to the lions.

As a result of such cases, ministers, churches and even lay workers in churches are having to purchase malpractice insurance.

It's a sad commentary on the shape of the world.

Just as medical doctors have grown leery of dealing with accident victims who might in turn bite the hand that heals them, so Christian leaders are being reminded that what looks like a wounded sheep may be a snapping wolf instead.

This is especially true with churches which deal with people coming off the street. Some people, it seems, are deliberately baiting ministers to force them to make a mistake so they can sue.

The immunity which was once afforded Christians, the winking way the world used to handle "ministerial exaggerations," is no longer available. One mistake, and the world is ready to take the Christian to court.

And feed him to the lions if possible.

For example, Dr. Thomas Harris, author of the widely read book on transactional analysis, *I'm O.K., You're O.K.*, sued Bible teacher Larry Tomczak for $19.5 million.

Tomczak, speaking at a Jesus rally in Chico, California, several years ago, repeated a widespread rumor that the aging California psychiatrist had committed suicide. His remarks were taped and later played over radio KFIA near Sacramento — where Harris lives.

Harris, who allegedly admitted his bookings and royalties had dropped off, hired a Los Angeles public relations firm, called a press conference, posed for pictures for *People* magazine and announced he was suing Tomczak for slander.

His new book, it seemed, was almost ready for publication.

But what many thought was just a publicity gag to get his name before a national audience turned into a nightmare for Tomczak

— and several others.

Although Harris's suicide had been rumored for years in secular circles, the suit seemed directed expressly at Christians. Also named were Bible teachers Jimmy Moore and Bob Mumford, from whom Tomczak allegedly heard his version of the rumor. Harris also sued the radio station, as well as the little tape ministry which duplicated the tapes.

What's to be learned? For one, despite what Shakespeare wrote, the world is not a stage — it is a battleground.

Christians must brace themselves against the heaviest onslaught in history as this age draws to a close.

Second, our mistakes will rise up to haunt us. Thus Paul's strong word to walk "circumspectly," or without blame, before the world is especially apropos.

While "they" won't put us in jail (at least not yet) for preaching the gospel, rest assured they will nail us to the tree for just one mistake.

Finally, if there ever was a time to pray for the gift of discernment of spirits, it is now. Too much of what seems harmless has been booby-trapped by Satan. The wise Christian must be careful of what he picks up.

A lot of things are exploding these days. Only, in this case, the lion is setting traps.

Fifty-five

IF YOUR PASTOR GETS A DIVORCE, CONTINUE TO LOVE AND MINISTER TO HIM

IN THE last few years at least two dozen well-known ministers — many of them my personal friends — have gone through divorce.

Some have stayed with their churches or perhaps moved to other churches. Others have taken on a traveling ministry so they will not have to listen to the muted echoes of the past.

Some have gone into secular work. A few have turned their backs on God.

All are sad cases.

The Episcopal priest who pointed me toward the Holy Spirit left his wife and married another woman. When I share my testimony, I am reluctant to mention his name, even though I love him dearly.

That hurts.

One of the nation's best-known evangelists said he had to choose between his wife and the ministry. It did not seem to occur to him that his wife was his ministry. He, too, has remarried and has continued to defend his position.

I think of the director of the family relations department of one of the nation's largest denominations who divorced his wife and married a younger woman. I still correspond with his former wife. She prays daily for her ex-husband.

The pastor of a large church recently stepped before his congregation and told them, in tears, that his wife had left him for another man.

And when the ministerial home of the president's pastor in Washington, D.C., fell to pieces in front of the national media, it seemed no one was immune.

The conflict and horror of divorce are far removed from my life today. My home is happy. It's difficult, in fact, to remember that just a few years ago my own home was a seething volcano of strife and jealousy — ready to explode.

How easy it is for me to judge — coldly and harshly — some of my fellow ministers who have not come through their battles as well as I, those who capitulated and sought divorce.

It's not my intent to analyze the reasons behind these divorces. However, there are some kingdom principles which pastors need to remember when evaluating their relationships with their divorced peers — and when leading their sheep in relating to wounded shepherds.

First, few people recognize the extreme pressures brought against the families of those in public ministry. A recent Knight-Ridder survey shows one out of twenty-five clergy marriages ends in divorce. Not bad, considering that almost one out of two ordinary marriages winds up that way.

But when a shepherd falls, the entire community knows — as they seem to know about everything that goes on in the parsonage.

The biggest contributing factor: involvement with a person of the opposite sex. A Methodist survey found that nine of every ten clergy divorces involved infidelity — and that in nearly every case the minister, rather than his (or her) spouse, was the offender.

Pastors need to remember (for they are often the hardest critics of brother pastors) that the shepherd is "on the point" in spiritual warfare. Satan knows that if he can strike the shepherd the sheep will scatter. If he can shoot down a chief, the warriors will fall into confusion.

So every satanic gun is trained on the minister. If he does not fall through immorality, he often falls by judging others who are immoral.

When a soldier is shot down in battle, we bring him home, pay his hospital bills, decorate him with medals, give him honor and restore him to service after he has a chance to heal — physically, mentally and emotionally.

But let some shepherd, lured from the safety of his fold by a tempting siren who claims she needs ministry, get lost in a maze of emotions and do crazy things — and we cast him out of the kingdom.

A friend of mine laments: The army of the Lord is the only one that shoots its wounded.

Why, we need to ask, is a confessed murderer more welcome in our pulpits than a divorced shepherd?

Second, we have no clear scriptural guidelines on this matter. Even the finest Bible scholars argue the points of divorce, remarriage and the place of the fallen minister. In fact, it was one of the burning issues when the scribes broached the subject with Jesus. And it is a subject modern Pharisees still love to debate.

Jesus never intended for man to use the Scriptures as a hammer and chisel to chip out a set of rules by which we can imprison one another. When Jesus discussed divorce, it was not to major on the exceptions, but to drive home the purpose of God in establishing the permanency of the home.

What sadness there must be in heaven when God hears His shepherds — those He has left in charge of the sheep — using the Scriptures as rocks with which to stone one another, rather than stones to build the church of God.

Third, a distinction must be made between those who divorce, those who divorce and later remarry, and those who divorce in order to remarry.

Divorce is the result of sin. It is the public admission of failure. Remarriage, however, is a different situation, for it closes the door on reconciliation. And divorce in order to remarry is specifically condemned in the Scriptures and may be the line a man crosses whereby he disqualifies himself for public ministry.

Fourth, more is required of those ordained to public ministry than ordinary men and women. Perhaps this is why shepherds are so hard on other shepherds who fall.

The question is asked: Does God judge His pastors with a different standard from the one He uses to judge those who follow?

The answer is *yes*. James says: "Not many of you should presume to be teachers, my brothers, because you know that we who teach will be judged more strictly" (James 3:1).

I confess I do not know the absolutes of that standard, or whether the standard is the same for all men. I suspect it is not. I suspect God judges each man, each woman, differently. I also suspect His standard of justice, or His standard of mercy, is unlike anything we comprehend in our feeble understanding of the Word.

At the same time, a man does not have to become a shepherd. He chooses to do so. And in so choosing he closes the door forever on the right to have his own way — even in marriage. By entering the ministry he disqualifies himself to be judged as a sheep.

Paul asks Timothy: "If anyone does not know how to manage his own family, how can he take care of God's church?" (1 Tim. 3:5).

It is a valid question, one which every responsible shepherd needs to answer. Perhaps it holds the answer to why we must not relax the standards of personal and domestic fidelity — and divine order in the home.

Yet when sin enters the ministry — and the minister — and batters him down into the dirt, we often find it easier to cover the wounded man with leaves and pretend the situation never existed than to deal with it openly and in love.

We don't like our prophets to raise their skirts and reveal feet of clay. It's easier for us to see only their smiling faces in the pulpit or listen to their teaching tapes. And to ignore their personal lives. But even though we have responsibilities to each other and cannot ignore each other's frailties, we must learn to recognize without condemning.

And that is most difficult when we all have some of the same tendencies in ourselves.

It is tragic, but sheep often minister to wounded shepherds — licking their wounds and snuggling close to provide warmth — far better than other shepherds, who debate the degrees of wrongness rather than provide healing to shepherds who need it.

The question is not divorce. It is not even divorce and remarriage. The question is repentance. Has the shepherd repented? Or is he arrogant and stubborn, declaring his rightness in the situation? Finding fault with those who fail to understand? Quoting

Scripture to back up his fallen position?

Repentance clears the deck for forgiveness and restoration. Arrogance disqualifies a man, whether he is divorced or not.

Fifth, every pastor who sees another pastor fall should remind himself, "There but for the grace of God, go I." It is easy to forget how things were or to overlook how they might have been in your own life except for the mercy of God.

In examining what Augustine calls the *felix culpa*, which loosely translated means "the happy sin," an interesting question is raised. Does God allow certain men to commit sin (or "fall into sin" if you are looking for a more passive phrase to ease your guilt) in order to stimulate the crisis experiences necessary to bring them to maturity?

Does God allow a man to sin? Even more radical, does God allow a sinful situation for the purpose of increasing the shaking and hastening maturity? Although my theology does not make room for this, it sure seems like it. And if so, it is certainly reason for the rest of us to give thanks that God has spared us from such harsh chastisement.

Shepherds are on the point, and as a result they are often the first to step on the land mines or to stumble into the snare of the enemy. In the process, new men are raised up. Old ones stagger, much wiser and more compassionate, to the rear lines for bandages and crutches in order to take new places in the army and fulfill the purpose of God.

I remember sitting in the kitchen of one of America's most famous television ministers, listening in shocked silence as he treated his wife in an almost subhuman way. Later that night he appeared on TV talking about his happy home. It is happy for him, I thought. Hell for her.

But despite their battles, this pastor and his wife stuck it out. They may have come close to killing each other, but they never considered divorce as a valid option. As a result they have now emerged in splendid unity.

What about "biblical reasons" for divorce? we ask. Does that not clear the innocent party?

Not always. The husband or wife who chooses to divorce because the mate has committed adultery was probably looking for a legalistic reason out of the marriage anyway.

Adultery is never a reason for divorce — merely an excuse.

When a man and woman become "one in Christ," nothing — not even adultery — can separate them.

Granted, there are times when divorce is the only way out. And until I have walked in another man's shoes, I must withhold judgment of him.

In my determination not to lower my own standards, I must never lower the standard on the head of the fallen brother to crush him under the law. The standard has only one purpose — to give a goal for restoration. It is not a reason for rejection.

Finally, in searching the guidelines for how to relate to divorced pastors, other shepherds need to apply the principles of Matthew 18.

Unfortunately, there is something in most of us that enjoys a juicy story — especially if it is about a well-known person.

Yet we seldom enjoy hearing gossip about our mothers, our fathers or our own children. Being a member of the family makes a difference.

Are we not commanded to love fellow pastors as members of one family?

Some time ago I entered into a covenant with a group of Christian leaders. We promised not to talk about each other until we had first talked to the accused party. This has been difficult. But the principle is sound, and I have endeavored to stick to it.

Then last year I heard that a man I deeply love and respect had left his wife and moved into an apartment. His church was falling apart. His sheep were scattering.

So I phoned him. Was it so? Yes! And I caught the brokenness of his heart. He needed not only my counsel; he needed my love.

Until I called him, I had been flooded with opinions. I had wanted to cry out: "Look what you are doing to the kingdom." But as we talked, I softened.

He had done wrong. But I would leave that in God's hands. And as to the kingdom? Well, it has weathered bigger things than this.

It survived the adultery and murder contract put out by King David.

It continued after John Wesley's wife stood in her husband's meetings and shouted, "Don't believe my husband. He is a hypocrite and a fraud."

The kingdom needs no defense. But kingdom pastors need the

prayers of other kingdom pastors — especially when they fall.

Thus, I have concluded it is not my job to condemn. I shall leave that to the legalists and those too insecure to love.

It is my task to bind the wounds of the fallen, to give sight to blind eyes, to open the prison doors of self-condemnation and, through prayer, pluck back my brothers and sisters from the snare of the enemy, as brands plucked from the fire.

True, a man's effectiveness as pastor is badly damaged when his failures explode into public view. It is hard to believe a man who says Christ can solve all your problems — and then confesses with his life that his problem is too big for Jesus.

It is hard to follow a man who says to "take up the cross" when he cannot bear his own cross.

Who among all God's pastors is qualified to cast the first stone? A man's ministry, like a man's servant, is the Master's business.

And it has been my personal experience that the justice of God is quick and sure. The Holy Spirit still lays a sharp ax at the root of every tree which dares stand and proclaim itself as a leader in the spiritual forest.

Does God remove His anointing when a man of God sins, or fails in marriage? Is it not possible that in the prison cells of condemnation and failure there stand once-shorn Samsons, their hair growing, praying that God will give them just one more chance to stand and glorify His name?

God forbid that I, by anything I say, should stand in the way of His restoration.

The question is not divorce, or even morality. The question is whether there is a call from God on a man's life. Because if a man has the call of shepherd, the sheep will hear his voice and follow.

Even if he walks with a limp.

Fifty-six

MUST GIFTED TEACHERS STAY HOME — OR CAN THE ABUSES BE CORRECTED?

A FRIEND of mine, an extraordinary teacher who travels extensively as well as having local responsibilities, declared last week that he was now refusing all invitations to speak away from home.

He said he was tired of people calling and saying, "Will you come speak to our group? We sure can *use* you."

The speaker leaves his family and local responsibilities to travel great distances. He arrives to find he is scheduled for the three evening services as agreed, but he is also supposed to:

• Speak to a local service club. ("Please don't mention Jesus because it will offend the Jews, and don't talk about the gifts of the Spirit because the Baptist pastor will be there.")

• Talk to a third-grade class in the local Christian school.

• Pray over the loudspeaker at the Friday afternoon junior high track meet.

• Speak to "the ladies" for three mornings at the church.

• Travel to a nearby town to have tea with the grandmother of the former pastor, who always has tea with the visiting minister.

All in all, he speaks nine times; counsels fourteen women who have already been counseled by their husbands, the pastor and the last five visiting speakers; and spends three nights in the bedroom of the pastor's five-year-old child so the church won't have to foot the motel bill.

If the speaker has *chutzpah*, he reminds someone he had to purchase his own airline ticket. If he is shy, he may wind up paying for it from his own pocket.

During the services he suffers through the "love offerings," gritting his teeth as the people are told the money will go to the visiting minister. He knows from experience that he will receive only a small amount. The rest will be spent by the local group on expenses or will go in the bank in case there's not enough to give the next visiting speaker.

It's no wonder my friend says he's not going out again. He's tired of being used.

Because of such insensitive abuses on the part of churches and other Christian organizations, an alarming number of America's finest teachers are doing what my friend has done. They are saying no to nearly all requests.

Others, especially those who travel full-time, have often been forced to commercialize their ministries. This is even more tragic.

Now we face the specter of the contemporary prophet and his booking agency which handles his schedule and demands a financial guarantee before the speaker will agree to come.

One wonders if Amos would have been effective as he prophesied against those who "lie upon beds of ivory" if he had first signed a contract with Amaziah for three thousand shekels before coming to speak.

When a minister — even if he is under great pressure by the abuses — puts his schedule in the hands of a booking agent, he can no longer be classified as a prophet or teacher. Now he is simply a commodity or, at best, a celebrity.

In order to obtain the services of these celebrities, the purchasers are forced to sign his contract, which spells out every detail of things to be done for his comfort and convenience. This often includes first-class air travel, fresh fruit in the motel room, a king-sized bed and a rental car at his disposal (Buick or better).

The Happy Booker sends his client where the calendar demands — with little thought to intense prayer, submission of the schedule to the concerned brothers or even consideration of God's will. The client is booked where he will draw the largest offerings and can sell his books, records and tapes (and add names to his mailing list for future solicitations). Or he is booked simply because he has a vacant Thursday night. (After all, it doesn't make sense to have a potential money-maker sitting idle in a motel room between engagements.)

Instead of being used, the celebrity is using the sponsoring group. One well-known celebrity demands six thousand dollars per sermon — and gets it. A famous singing group upped its demands last year to ten thousand dollars a performance. Other musical groups make even more ridiculous demands, including chauffeur-driven limousines and fresh flowers for the ladies.

It's sad. How do we achieve balance?

First, we recognize there is a place for the traveling speaker and minstrel. While 2 John warns against hospitality to those who speak simply for monetary gain, 3 John encourages churches and sponsoring groups to be hospitable to those who go from place to place ministering in the name of the Lord.

Second, the sponsoring group should trust God for a "double portion" to honor the visiting minister. If that does not come through the love offering, it should come out of the pockets of the sponsors. Such are the risks of daring to say, "God told me to invite you."

If a love offering is received for the visiting minister, every dime should go to the minister. If the sponsoring group intends to use only a portion of the offering as an honorarium, the visiting minister should be told in advance, and the audience should be told the same thing before they give. The truth sets us free.

Third, the visiting minister should be willing to trust God to supply his need. Thus, if the Lord told him to accept a certain invitation, he should then be willing to cover his own expenses if necessary.

Personally, I feel churches and sponsoring groups should refuse invitations to speakers and musicians who demand a guarantee. It's frightening to think you might pay for — and get — some Samson dressed in an exciting wig but shorn of the Spirit.

Let's go only where God says go, regardless of tantalizing rewards from other sectors. Let's invite only those God says invite, even if they have never been on national TV. The crowds may be small, but the Holy Spirit has a way of showing up at meetings like that.

What else matters?

Fifty-seven

WHO'S OUTRAGED? NOT ME!

CONCERNED THAT the government was trying to indoctrinate his son with anti-biblical beliefs, a Louisiana state senator, Bill Keith, got a law passed in 1981 requiring the state's public school teachers to tell students both sides of creation theory. That meant if the science lesson mentioned evolution, the teacher was forced by law to teach creation science also.

What is creation science? It is the teaching that a supernatural being created not only this earth, but also created the species separately and that no living thing can change (evolve) from one form into another. Specifically, it teaches that human beings did not evolve from lower creatures but were created in the image of God.

Do I believe that? Of course. It's impossible to believe the Bible is true without believing God is the Creator. I believed it long before I knew there was some kind of movement called the "creationist movement." I believed it because it is true. Not only that, it makes sense.

On June 19, 1987, however, the U.S. Supreme Court in a landmark decision struck down the law passed in 1981. The response was similar to that which takes place when a workman in the fireworks factory flips his cigarette into a box of cherry bombs.

Speaking from the far left, Steve Shapiro of the American Civil Liberties Union hailed the decision as "a legal end to the creationism movement."

On the other side, conservative presidential aspirant Pat Robertson said, "Everyone in America who believes he or she was created by God will be outraged. The Supreme Court has written into the Constitution a questionable scientific theory of the origin of life."

Who's right?

Not Shapiro. As long as men believe the Bible, they will believe God created this earth and the people who dwell on it. In fact, even in lands where there is no Bible, people believe God created this earth because God has done more than write a Bible — He also writes on the hearts of men. No U.S. Supreme Court ruling will change who created this earth, nor will it change what people believe.

Do I agree with Pat Robertson? Usually, but not this time. His law degree should make him able to understand legal opinions. But having to say the right political thing often gets in the way of truth. Robertson and his conservatives surely realize the court's ruling had nothing to do with whether God created this earth or not. God is capable of providing all the proof He needs for that. Nor did the court declare evolution to be the American way. It simply said you cannot force a teacher to teach certain theories.

Although Keith's bill was carefully written to promote academic freedom without religious overtones, it was clearly a subterfuge to bring the Bible back to the classroom. As such it violated the Constitution's requirement of separation between government and religion.

The writers of the Constitution added the First Amendment to prevent the church from being oppressive as it had been in England. There the king, who was also head of the church, used a cruel government to force his theology on the people. Our founding fathers determined it should not happen here.

Therefore, I was not outraged at the court's ruling. It was proper. The court did not forbid teachers from telling children that God created the world and created each species separately. That's allowed. What's not allowed is a law that demands it. The well-meaning people in Louisiana, who were trying to protect themselves from godless humanism, were using the wrong method.

In 1962 the court ruled that the state of New York was wrong in requiring all children to recite written prayers in the classrooms. However, despite what our president and others say about prayer being forbidden in the classrooms, Justice Hugo Black, in writing the majority opinion, stated: "Students have the right to practice prayer and read the Bible. But they do not have the right to the aid of the state in that exercise."

The following year Madalyn Murray O'Hair was party to an auxiliary case when the court ruled that governmentally required religious devotionals violated the Constitution. Then, as now, church people became paranoid — not stopping to realize the government had not prohibited prayers in the classrooms. The court said enforced prayers — whether written by Hindus, satanists or Christians — were wrong. In fact, one year later a federal judge in New Jersey used that ruling to deny supporters of transcendental meditation from teaching their doctrine in the public schools.

The church is composed of people "called out" of the world. We do not depend on good laws for help, nor are we hampered by bad laws. We are part of a different kingdom. Why get uptight when our highest court rules on any law? If carnal parents and a lazy church depend upon public schools to teach our children that God created this earth, we've already departed from God's method. Rather than battle for new laws, why not elect Christians to the school boards and go to work evangelizing the nation's school teachers?

At no time did Jesus encourage His disciples to petition Rome. He told them to petition God. The one man who did petition Rome, Paul, got what Rome gives — death. Even if our government does become oppressive, God's power is best seen in a hostile environment.

Perhaps, rather than having us trust in Washington, He wants us to trust in Him.

Fifty-eight

THE BOOK RACKS
OF BAAL

A SAD thing is happening in our land. More and more gifted writers are dipping their golden goblets, once dedicated for sacred use, into the wine of pornography.

As a result most secular book racks now have the flavor of Belshazzar's feast rather than the healthy food once served up by the literary chefs of America.

Pornography is nearly always badly written and carries no message other than the single purpose of achieving erotic and momentary stimulation.

It is also a cheap counterfeit of the real thing.

Real men and women don't look the way the pornographers portray them.

Our stomachs pooch, breasts sag and veins extend. Underneath our cosmetics, braces, supports, girdles, bras, toupees, dentures, glasses, deodorants, sprays, powders and fitted clothing we are not erotic bodies. Rather we are human souls created in a variety of shapes designed to love, to be loved and to glorify God.

Pornography is never graphic — it is twisted and distorted. Actually there is far more truth and beauty in a cattle-breeding pen than in today's porn. It is by and large without art and creativity — depicting only the emptiness of the soul.

But, as the writers have learned, it is a sure way to sell books.

However, it is when pornography is combined with talent that it becomes most profane.

In my own search for excellence in literary forms I finally decided to read a Harold Robbins book. Robbins, you see, is not the run-of-the-mill, pant-and-groan porn writer. He is a man of great literary talent. His publisher calls him — without apology — "the world's best storyteller."

No small claim that.

It is at that point the sounds of Belshazzar's feast are heard. Here is a man of vast talent who has taken his marvelous gift — the gift of storytelling — and married his bride to the lecherous debauchery of pornography.

What a sad, sad waste.

Robbins is not alone. Philip Roth, Gore Vidal, Gay Talese, Erica Jong — all have profaned the golden goblet of storytelling, a gift Jesus used so beautifully in His parables.

The human body, clothed or unclothed, remains the temple of the Holy Spirit. It is the object for which our Lord bore stripes to heal. It is sad when that body is exploited and defamed.

Even sadder is the world in which these writers live — a world so full of hedonism and spiritual emptiness that the God of the universe, the only sure and certain factor in life and death, is totally ignored.

God does not judge men on their outer appearance, rather on their inner being. It is here we discover the sickness and emptiness of those who write. Their world, sadly, is weighed on the size of their bank accounts and the sexual organs of their characters.

Weighed in the balances, I add, and found wanting.

I am angered, however, when talented, gifted men and women use their gifts to depict the symbols of God and holy things to heighten eroticism. Egged on by reviewers, television hosts, and other flotsam and jetsam in the cesspool of pseudo literature, these writers glibly promote their own homosexuality and demonic perversions without even the artistic modesty of a fig leaf.

Surely to take the gift of storytelling — a gift so many of us cherish for the purpose of communicating holy truth — and use that gift to entice young and old alike into the pit of hedonism rather than to challenge the reader to yearn for the beauty of holiness — surely that is the most hideous of blasphemy.

God understands biology. He called our body functions good. They are for health and enjoyment. However, the barren spirit is still as cursed as the fruitless fig tree.

There are many excellent contemporary novels on the secular market. The *New York Times* called Walter Wangerin's *The Book of the Dun Cow* "far and away the most literate and intelligent story of the year." I agree.

There are many great storytellers with high purposes. Jack Higgins, Arthur Hailey, Piers Paul Reid, James Michener — all are gifted writers.

But like eating from a can of contaminated food, I have dipped for the last time into the poisoned world of Harold Robbins.

"Why," the prophet asked, "spend money on what is not bread? Eat what is good, and your soul will delight..." (see Is. 55:2).

Perhaps Robbins is the *world's* best storyteller. However, the crayon-scribbled message of a Sunday school child, the strivings of a Christian writer whose manuscript is turned down again and again for publication — anything written for the glory of God — ranks that writer as greater in the kingdom of God than all the Robbinses, Roths and Jongs combined.

To my Christian writer friends I say: Never settle for mediocrity. Strive always for excellence. But do not judge your success on the number of books you sell. Write for God's glory, and your two mites dropped unnoticed in the treasury will be counted as far more than all those expensive sacrifices offered on the book racks of Baal and mammon.

Fifty-nine

CHOOSING
TO OBEY GOD

I WAS fresh out of seminary and the new pastor of a Baptist church in a little South Carolina town when Martin Luther King led his famous march from Montgomery to Selma, Alabama. We did a lot of talking about racial segregation in our deacons' meetings those days. Everyone was defensive.

"We're integrated," one man said. "When Miss Jessie died, we allowed her maid to come to the funeral and sit in the balcony along with her pickaninny."

Not too far away, in Greensboro, North Carolina, four black college students refused to move from a Woolworth's lunch counter when denied service. It was 1961. By September more than seventy thousand students, whites and blacks, had participated in sit-ins.

Our deacons appointed a special committee to patrol the street in front of the church in case "the darkies" tried to get in. "They got their own churches," Harry Lemwood, a grocer, used to say. "Let 'em go there."

I groaned over the injustice, but when King marched on Selma, I did not join him — even though I knew he was right. I didn't even stand up in my pulpit and applaud him. I kept silent.

I wasn't afraid of Bull Conner. Or the snarling police dogs. Or of being put in jail. What I feared most was losing my "job" as pastor. I preached against segregation, which was acceptable because of King's sacrifice. But I knew better than to *do* anything rash, like marching. I just stayed home and preached the gospel.

I quoted Romans 13 — that Christians should not break the law — to justify my stance. No matter that the law said blacks were inferior to whites. No matter that it was cruel, dehumanizing and anti-Christ. It was the law. By isolating Romans 13 from the rest of the Bible, I justified legalized sin.

Today I still feel guilty for not marching.

All this came to mind a while back when I talked with my friend Guy Strayhorn, an attorney from Fort Myers, Florida. Guy had just returned from Atlanta, where he took part in one of the Operation Rescue demonstrations at an abortion clinic.

As a member of the bar Guy is sworn to uphold the law. But which law? In this case he believed there was a direct conflict between God's law and man's law.

He went to Atlanta in the spirit of Shiphrah and Puah, the Hebrew midwives who deliberately disobeyed the Egyptian pharaoh when ordered to kill Hebrew baby boys. Yet by breaking the law they saved the lives of innocent babies — including one named Moses.

Civil disobedience. Or, as James Dobson calls it, spiritual obedience.

Guy went to Atlanta because he believes unborn babies are human beings. He went for the same reason I should have gone to Selma — to protest national evil.

In choosing to obey God rather than man he paid the same price Daniel paid — who was thrown into a den of lions; the same price Peter and John paid — who were arrested and beaten badly.

Changes for good come because men like Martin Luther King and Guy Strayhorn take a stand.

How easy it is for us modern-day priests and Levites to quote Scripture that justifies inaction.

Jesus not only advocated civil disobedience; He practiced it by disobeying Jewish law, which was the law of the land. Yet this was not His primary means of effecting change. Real change came when Jesus took spiritual authority over the demonic forces that put men in bondage.

Although I applaud Operation Rescue for drawing attention to the horror of mass abortion, the battle will not be won on the curbs of America. Protests and demonstrations will not sway the U.S. Supreme Court. Their decision will be based on each justice's interpretation of the U.S. Constitution. A godly interpretation is now possible. But bank on this — Satan will throw all the powers of hell at the justices to confuse their minds.

The real struggle is against what Paul calls "the spiritual forces of evil in the heavenly realms." American Christians — through fasting and prayer — can push those forces back, allowing the justices to hear from God, for some of them are praying people.

So what should I do? Sit on a curb in front of an abortion clinic? Yes, but only if God tells me to. However, I don't have to ask about spiritual warfare. That I must do. That I will do.

Sixty

THE SPIRIT
OF MURDER

O NE EARLY morning in January the lights in the Florida State Penitentiary flickered and dimmed as the executioner pulled a switch in the death chamber. More than four thousand volts of electricity surged through the body of Ted Bundy, who was strapped in the three-legged oak electric chair known as Old Sparky. Bundy, who may have murdered more than fifty people, jerked against the restraining straps — then slumped to one side. Whiffs of smoke came from under his hood, his wrists and his legs where the electrodes were attached. Justice was done.

Yet the scene outside the death chamber was evidence that while one murderer was dead, the spirit of murder lives on. It was alive and active in the more than two hundred people who had gathered in the early morning darkness to celebrate Bundy's execution.

As the funeral hearse pulled away from the prison, people hooted, jeered and held up obscene signs reading, "Burn, Bundy, Burn" and "Roast in Peace."

The fact that Ted Bundy may have deserved to die did not justify the wild glee that his execution stirred up. What scares me even more is that I sometimes see that same spirit in the faces of church people.

That same month I published an article in *Ministries Today* titled "The Manipulative Strategy of a Child Molester." It was written by a former pastor who had spent more than ten years in prison for fondling little girls. It was an articulate but frightening warning to church leaders, telling them how to spot the kind of person he used to be.

I say used to be, for he's no longer a child molester. He's one of the few men I know who have been genuinely rehabilitated in prison. A college and seminary graduate with a loving wife and children, he had pastored one of the larger churches in his state before his sin was discovered. Arrested, shamed and convicted, he was sentenced to forty years in prison. During that time he went through extensive treatment. He came to grips not only with his sin and crimes but with himself. He genuinely repented. He sought and received deliverance. After being turned down several times by the parole board, some of us went to bat for him. He was finally released. The day he walked out of prison his wife, who had stuck with him through the entire ordeal, served him with divorce papers. She was too afraid, too wounded, to risk it again. If he was to start over, he would do it alone.

A Pentecostal family took him in, gave him a job and introduced him to the life in the Spirit. It's tough going. Although he'll never pastor another church, he's making it — as a man and as a victorious Christian.

The article, which I asked him to submit, was his first, hesitant step in trying to help others. "If leaders can be warned how to spot people like I was," he told me through tears, "maybe innocent children can be spared the agony of molestation."

For obvious reasons we did not use his name with the story.

Reaction was radical. Some wrote commending us. In others, strange spirits reacted. One pastor wrote the angriest letter I've ever gotten in response to an article: "The author needs to be shot — executed. He is not worthy to live and menace other little girls.... You printed a deviant's operations, with not a word of where he is. He does not deserve to live, and society is quickly tiring of his ilk. If judges don't carry through with executions, the public will take it into their own hands. Count on it!"

I wrote back, telling the pastor the reason we did not identify the author was to protect him from men like him.

It doesn't take a psychologist to realize that anyone who reacts with such violence is possessed not only with the same spirit that caused the author to molest children, but a spirit of murder.

I've seen that same spirit sweep across the faces in an audience when I'm preaching and attack some social evil. At a recent conference I preached against abortion. The reaction frightened me as I sensed a lynch mob spirit just beneath the surface of Christian veneer. They not only hated abortion; they hated the abortionists.

Sitting in the back of a crusade meeting several years ago, I listened as a preacher whipped the crowd into a fury as he attacked everything from the Catholic church to pornography. As each new verbal attack was launched against one of these groups, the crowd would rise to its feet, and the people would shout their support. I could hear the hate in their loud "Amen!" These people were being transformed. They could feel the power of the spirit of murder — and they liked it.

The truth is, we've made sin and sinner synonymous and, incredibly, exempted ourselves from both categories.

It's bad enough to live in a world where people jeer at hearses, blast their horns at traffic lights and fire guns into automobiles on the freeway. But when this same syndrome infects the church, it's time to grow fearful.

I wanted to hate Ted Bundy. But I couldn't. One reason is that I have a friend, a Spirit-filled brother, who is one of those next in line to be roasted in Old Sparky. I love him dearly, and I'm grieved. He is why I'm now struggling with capital punishment.

Love, I've discovered, leaves no room for vengeance.

Sixty-one

WOULD JESUS
PULL THE
SWITCH?

O N DECEMBER 23, 1973, a twenty-year-old Carl Songer, high on drugs, shot and killed a state trooper who had found him sleeping in the back of a stolen car.

Justice was quick. Within weeks Carl had been convicted of first-degree murder and sentenced to die in Florida's electric chair. For sixteen years he awaited his execution on death row in the state penitentiary.

When John Spenkelink, the first man to be executed by Florida, went to the electric chair, he left his Bible with Carl Songer. Carl, who had been raised in a poor but God-fearing home, put the Bible on a shelf in his cell. It seemed irrelevant to his situation. Why was he on death row when others, who had committed far worse crimes, were being paroled — or acquitted? Why did those who had money to hire expensive lawyers seem to get out of prison, while the blacks, mentally retarded and poor whites like him rotted away in dismal existence?

The wheels of justice continued their slow grind toward the death chamber. Three times the governor of Florida signed his death warrant. Each time Carl was transferred from his cell on death row to a small cell called the "death watch cell" thirty feet from the execution chamber. Each time the appeals courts granted stays, and Carl was returned to death row.

One evening, seven years after being convicted, Carl was sitting on the edge of his bunk staring at the floor when suddenly he was aware of a "light" in his cell, above and behind his head.

"When I tried to look up and see what it was, it moved back. I knew it was more than a light. It was a presence."

Confused and afraid, Carl sat immobile. The light returned, resting just above his head.

"God," the condemned prisoner whispered, "is that You?"

Instantly the light swept down in front of his eyes and, in a silent explosion, entered his chest. Carl Songer dropped his head into his hands and wept.

The weeping continued for three days. During this time he relived, in vivid detail, the events of his past life. He realized he had bought the arguments used by his defense lawyers — that he was not guilty. That he was a victim of drugs. That society was really to blame.

However, the light would not allow that. Now he saw himself the way he really was. Without cause he had taken the life of a woman's husband, a child's father, a mother's son. He was a sinner. He was a murderer.

Somehow Carl Songer related this to the Bible. Although his parents were members of a little Baptist church, he had not been to church since he was a child. He opened the book, but it didn't make sense. Then he came to the Gospel of John: "In the beginning was the Word, and the Word was with God, and the Word was God" (1:1, KJV).

"Jesus," Carl whispered. He said the name again and again, louder and louder. Jesus was God. It was Jesus who had come into his cell and entered his body and spirit. He had been filled with the Spirit of Jesus.

For the next several years Carl devoured the Bible. Then he received a letter. Lisa Crews, who had sat on the jury that convicted and sentenced him, had become a Christian. She was in our church. When she heard the governor had signed a fourth death warrant, she wrote to ask Carl's forgiveness and to share her faith in Jesus.

Carl wrote back. He forgave her for her part in his situation and told her of his own experience with God — an ever-growing relationship that had given him unbelievable strength when he last faced the electric chair.

Lisa sent him several of my books. Then Carl wrote me. Would I be willing to come up, stay with him in his cell the night before he was to be killed, then witness the execution?

I made several trips to see him. I was with him the week before his scheduled execution. I met his parents, poor but godly people who had driven their pickup truck to Florida so they could return his body to Oklahoma for a "Christian burial."

I enlisted my church in prayer, and, ten hours before he was to be executed, the Supreme Court granted another stay.

That was several years ago. Few things have shaken me as that experience. I had always been a passive believer in capital punishment. But this time it was evident the state of Florida was killing the wrong man. The old Carl Songer had died nine years before. The man they planned to execute was a new creature.

I went to the Bible. While the levitical law calls for death, the prophets tell us of a different God. "I take no pleasure in the death of the wicked," Ezekiel quoted God, "but rather that they turn from their ways and live" (Ezek. 33:11).

Some ask, What if it was your son that he killed? But that's not the right question. The question is, What if it was my son who killed someone?

The basic question is not, Did Carl Songer deserve to die? No, we all deserve to die. The real question deals with Jesus. Would Jesus pull the switch? He came to fulfill the law of retribution with the higher law of transformation. The question that must be asked with capital punishment — as with all social issues — is, What would Jesus do?

The Supreme Court determined Carl should not be executed. They changed his sentence to life in prison. Even though he'll be behind bars for a long time, he's a free man. Set free from the law of sin and death by Jesus.

Sixty-two

A Tip
Worth
Taking

I T WAS Gandhi, legend has it, who said, "I would be a follower of Christ were it not for Christians."

A restaurant waitress from Pueblo, Colorado, struggling with that same problem, asked, "Why are Christians so rude to waitresses?"

Every place she had worked, she wrote, this was a hot topic among the waitresses. "Believe me, sir, I'd rather serve a party of drunks than a party of Christians — and I'm a Holy Ghost-filled Christian woman."

I sat reading her letter, imagining a group of waitresses standing in the kitchen talking about the loud, rude bunch of people who had just come in from a church meeting.

"Church people demand beyond reason — then they don't tip at all."

Well, she's right about that. I was with a man recently who, after sending his meal back twice because it wasn't cooked to his taste, punished the waitress by not leaving a tip. I could have lived with it, since he was paying the bill, had he not made a big deal of bowing his head and praying out loud before we ate — while the waitress stood to one side watching. After we got outside I excused myself, returned and gave her a double tip. I told her I was doing it for two reasons: One, because she had earned it for having to put up with my friend; two, because God wanted to bless her in a special way.

She cried.

I have a young friend who is raising a child as a single parent — working as a waitress at Denny's. She leaves for work at 5:30 A.M. — six days a week — in order to drop her baby off at the day-care center. She makes $3.25 an hour, the rest on tips. "Non-Christians tip best," she says. "Christians leave small tips and sometimes a gospel tract. Some don't even tip — especially breakfast.

"It's hard enough," she told me, "to go to church on the one day I don't have to work. But what really stinks is finding yourself behind the loudmouth who's always complaining that his coffee is cold, then leaves twenty-five cents — which I have to split with the busboy."

It seems stupid that I would use all this space to write about treating waitresses, and anybody else who works in a service job, like human beings. I mean, this world is burning down with problems. Drugs and abortion are destroying our nation. Humanism has taken over government, education, even the church. Islam is out to conquer the earth. Surely we've got more important things to discuss than the size of tips.

But it's more than the size of tips. It has to do with being kingdom citizens. When Gandhi went to South Africa after graduating from law school in England, his mind was open to receive the gospel. Instead, because his skin was brown, Christians treated him like trash. Who knows what massive changes in history would have occurred had Christians acted like Christ?

That's the reason I'm kind and generous to servers — waitresses, lawn-care workers, snow shovelers, garbage collectors, bag boys and cab drivers.

Many of these are working at minimum wage and depend on tips to make it. Christians should be the best tippers in the world. The Bible has more to say about giving to those in need than all the other kinds of giving combined.

Besides, whatever happened to being nice? Polite? Friendly? We live in a world of people who seldom say "thank you," "please" or "I'm sorry." Kingdom kids, of all people, should treat others — especially those who serve us — with love, dignity and generosity.

I've come from church services where the pastor greeted each person at the door as if he or she were the richest person on earth, but at the restaurant he wouldn't look the waitress in the face, much less grunt a thank-you for his food.

There's just a chance, you know, that one of these servants might be an angel on assignment. And how do you get around "if you do it to the least of these, you do it to Me"?

Last Sunday night I sat in a local restaurant with my wife. The corner booth next to us was filled with a happy, laughing group from another church. They kept the waitress, who was an elderly grandma-type, on the run. "More coffee. We're out of catsup. Can you bring more water? My hamburger is rare instead of well-done. My fried egg is hard." Never a kind word. Never a thank-you.

I sat there, looking across the table at Jackie and thinking, What if that were my widow waiting tables at night? Would God's people treat her like that? As you would that men should do unto your wife, so do you to the waitress...the checkout girl at the grocery store...the sales clerk.

Last winter I arrived at the Norfolk airport after midnight. There was snow on the ground and one lone cab at the curb. On the ride to the hotel God whispered, "Bless the driver for Me."

At the hotel I paid the fare, then handed him an extra twenty dollars. "God knows you're having a tough time. He asked me to give this to you on His behalf."

He sat, just staring at the bill. I hastened inside. I hate for strangers to see me cry.

Be generous with those who serve. God, I suspect, blesses tippers as well as tithers.

Sixty-three

On Being Sent Away From the Table

NORMAN VINCENT Peale tells the story of the time he decided to shock his mom by coming home from school one afternoon, parking his bike in the driveway and saying, "Damn it!" loud enough for her to know that he was now a man.

He says what she did to him shocked him a lot more than he had shocked her.

I grew up in a home like that. Bad language of any kind evoked instant punishment.

One night at the supper table I decided to impress the family with my machismo. I described a football injury suffered that afternoon at practice as hurting "like the devil." My dad reminded me that any reference to the devil was profane and sent me away from the table.

It was great vocabulary training, for it forced me — if I was going to eat with the family — to learn to be expressive without being vulgar.

Now it's not my dad who sends me from the table, it's editors and publishers (and a few vocal readers).

My first reaction to those who criticize my selection of words is usually bland. "I understand, Mr. Editor. The Pharisees rejected

Jesus also."

It's not until later that I become cynical.

However, it is sad that many evangelical Christians don't appreciate humor — especially the kind that pokes holes in pompous balloons.

Yet, while stiffness and stuffiness may be the problem of others, that does not excuse me from running my own self-inventory.

Why, for instance, do I sometimes insist on wearing tennis shoes to church?

Why do I love to play the role of the iconoclast?

Why, in the case of my column in an issue of *Charisma*, did I use a word which offended so many — one having to do with fungus?

In answer to that last question I've reached several conclusions:

(1) I used it to shock complacent readers. That's legitimate.

(2) I used it to draw attention to myself, to let people know I am a macho man. That's illegitimate.

(3) I used it to be funny. That's legitimate as long as the humor is a communicative technique.

It's unacceptable if I use humor because I am basically an insecure person who needs the acceptance of people's laughter.

Preachers are notorious for this. They often inject little "funnies" into their sermons. They'll make a point and then say, "HELLO! Anyone there?"

This brings titters of laughter.

Or, after a rousing plea for more humility, the preacher will ruin the whole thing by shouting, "AMEN? I said, 'AMEN?' " And keep it up until everyone is shouting, "AMEN!"

A famous Southern preacher used to wear red socks, sequined trousers and flashing checkered sport coat into the pulpit, then begin his message by praying, "O God, hide me behind the cross."

Even if God could have squeezed that fat fellow behind the cross, he still would have glowed like a neon sign.

Recently I sat on the platform behind a well-known charismatic preacher. I counted sixteen different gimmicks he used to awaken his congregation (and draw attention to himself).

Although he was preaching against worldliness — and especially against folks like me who use crude language now and then

— all I could see was his Hollywood coiffure, his expensive suit and a diamond ring that would impress even God.

Yet, despite his offensiveness to me — as I sat there in blue jeans and tennis shoes — he was doctrinally sound and communicated well with his audience. I was forced back to the words of the apostle Paul: "Who are you to judge another man's servant?"

If I argue that the Holy Spirit occasionally directs me to use a shock word, must I not allow this man the right to wear a huge diamond?

The point is this. If we are going to be ourselves, we must be prepared to offend others — and not become angry, cynical or feel rejected when it happens.

In the front of my Bible I have several notes penned to myself. One of them says, "Jamie, don't let the world (or the church) mold you into its image."

I intend to hold to that. But doing so means I run the risk, on occasion, of having my readers — or my editors — send me away from the table.

I don't mind, as long as you don't object to my giggling out there in the kitchen.

Part Ten

———

ON BUILDING
BRIDGES

Sixty-four

INTERCESSION

THE SUMMER after I graduated from high school, my father had surgery for a double hernia. The operation was performed in a small hospital in Asheville, North Carolina, near my parents' summer cabin in Hendersonville.

In those days it was customary to employ a private nurse because there were very few hospital staff nurses available. The surgeon recommended a mountain woman by the name of Julia Baldwin.

Julia was typical of the raw-boned, hard-working women who live in the Blue Ridge Mountains. She came into my father's room the morning he was to have surgery. "Praise the Lord," she said, grinning. "Let's pray!"

I was embarrassed. It was a critical time in my life. I was getting ready to leave for college. I wanted a relationship with God, but I was afraid of what that might mean. Now in walked this ruddy-faced, middle-aged woman — bubbling like Alka-Seltzer in water.

She assumed, when she heard I was enrolled in a Christian college, that I had a relationship with Jesus. "Come and visit my church," she said. "You'll love it."

There was no way to back out. The following Sunday, using my mother's car, I drove out to the little Christian and Missionary Alliance church. The service was just starting. The people were singing and clapping. I'd never heard this kind of music. Julia was in the choir. She saw me come in, grinned and waved, motioning me to join her. I was terrified. People turned and looked. Then, incredibly, she came down out of the choir loft and took my arm. Suddenly I was up there — singing and clapping my hands with the rest of the congregation.

I loved it! It was the first time in all my life I had been in a church service with vigor, and the people responded vocally — with even more vigor. I had only heard of folks who said, "Amen!" in church. Now I was surrounded by them. That morning of my eighteenth year, sitting in the little choir loft of a Christian and Missionary Alliance church, something sparked in my heart. This was what I had been looking for and didn't even know existed. I ventured out and said my first hesitant "Amen!" It felt good.

After church Julia took me to her house. I still remember the location on Merrimon Avenue. She fed me lunch and talked about God. She was the only person I'd ever met who talked about Him in the present tense. She was also the first person I had ever wanted to tell all the sins in my life.

As I was leaving, she gave me a book with a green dust jacket. It was called *Rees Howells, Intercessor*, by Norman Grubb. "It will save your life," she said.

I mumbled my embarrassed thanks and left. I waited nineteen years before I opened it. I had had an experience with the Holy Spirit and was eager for everything from God. Reading the life of Rees Howells convinced me that prayer was the key to the door of heaven. All things were mine if I prayed.

Incredibly, though, I did not keep on praying. I spent more time talking about God than I did talking to Him. Gradually, I was dying.

A diagnosis of cancer, however, has an amazing way of sorting priorities. Prayer, once again, became all important. Strangely, while my wife, family and thousands of people were praying for me, I found myself praying for others.

At night, as I lay in bed, the cancer raging in my gut, I prayed for those praying for me. My wife, sensing my urgency, joined me in intercession: in the early waking hours before we got out of bed...as we drove the car...sitting in the doctor's office...if we heard a siren...when word came of others with cancer...for missionaries...as God brought names to mind. Intercession became — and has remained — a life-style, just as it was for Rees Howells.

Following the miracle of healing, someone reminded me of Job 42:10 (KJV): "The Lord turned the captivity of Job, when he prayed for his friends." Intercession, it seems, often heals in both directions.

Early this morning, standing in front of my bookshelf, my fingers ran along the books and stopped on a green dust jacket, now ripped along the spine. I gently removed the book, holding it like an old, fragile friend. Scrawled in pencil on the cover page was a message written forty-one years ago. "God has great things for you — through prayer." It was signed Julia Baldwin.

Sixty-five

LIZZY'S MIRACLE

BACK AROUND Christmas, ten-year-old Lizzy Gross told her mother, Lestra, "Mommy, I'm seeing double."

That night Lestra mentioned it to her husband, Johnny, who is minister of music at Cornerstone Church in San Antonio, Texas. They prayed.

The parents continued to check Lizzy's eyes. The ophthalmologist, who originally diagnosed the condition as a lazy eye, recommended a pediatric ophthalmologist.

The specialist took one look. His voice reflected his alarm: "You need to see a neurologist."

The neurologist was kind but blunt. The possibility of a brain tumor was strong. He ordered a magnetic resonance imaging (MRI) scan of her brain.

That afternoon Johnny talked to his pastor, John Hagee. Hagee immediately called his ten-thousand-member Cornerstone Church into prayer.

Two days later Johnny received an emergency phone call at the church office. His face blanched white as he heard the MRI report.

"It couldn't be worse," he said with quivering voice. "The doctor says she shows an inoperable tumor in the center of her brain."

215

More tests followed. More doctors' visits. The Jewish neurologist sat the parents down. "I've seen this too many times. She'll be dead inside a year."

Lestra Gross, however, refused the verdict. In a letter to me, she said: "You would never give your children a book you wrote filled with promises, tell them that without faith in those promises it is impossible to please you, then watch them do what you asked and not honor their faith. Neither would God."

About this time John Hagee called me. Last summer John and his wife, Diana — along with the Cornerstone Church — had helped carry me in prayer when the doctors gave me similar news. He was calling the Cornerstone Church to fast and pray every Monday. Would our church pray also?

Lestra sent us a picture of Lizzy, which went up in our kitchen. Later she called, weeping. Diana had told her of the new cancer attack on my body. "Every time I pray for Lizzy, I pray for you."

A second MRI confirmed the tumor deep in Lizzy's brain. Treatment would destroy brain tissue, and a biopsy would be extremely risky.

By this time the iris and pupil in her eye had almost disappeared into her head. Only the white was showing. Her eyelids were drooping. Her face seemed to be losing its definition on one side.

A third MRI showed no significant change. A radiologist thought the tumor had even enlarged.

One day, as winter drew to a close, the school called. Lizzy was vomiting from a massive headache. Johnny ran into Hagee's office and fell into his arms.

"It's happening, just as the doctors said it would." It was the only time in the ordeal that fear took over.

Hagee prophesied: "You shall not let Satan replace faith with fear. This is not as it seems." He held his friend and prayed.

The next morning the church leaders gathered in the huge auditorium. They lay on the floor, praying for Lizzy. She returned to school the next day, her headache gone. The prayers intensified. Within ten days her eye was returning to normal.

"Does this condition sometimes get better before it gets worse?" Johnny asked the neurosurgeon.

"No," he answered, "she should be getting worse. Let's have another MRI."

Soon after the visit to her pediatric doctor, Hagee received a call from the Jewish neurologist involved in Lizzy's case. "We believed there was a brain tumor in the child's head. Now all the symptoms are gone. How could this be?"

After telling the doctor about the prayer and fasting, Hagee said, "Doctor, we pray to the same God you pray to, the God who heals all our diseases. Would you call this a miracle?"

"Well, if it's not a miracle, it's pretty close."

Hagee laughed. "Hang on to your yarmulke, doctor. You ain't seen nothing yet. *Baruch hashem!*" (Hebrew: "Blessed be God.")

The doctor paused. *"Baruch hashem,* pastor."

A month later, on April 26, Lizzy had a fourth MRI. All the symptoms of a brain tumor had disappeared, much to the doctors' amazement.

In June, Lizzy's neurologist admitted, "In all my twenty years of practice, this case comes the closest to where prayer actually seemed to work."

Yes, prayer does work.

Sixty-six

DUAL
STATUS

A GROWING number of us, I have discovered, have tasted heaven but returned to (or remained on) earth. We are the ones who have literally "entered into His presence."

Some have experienced that wonderful level of intimacy with God through prayer and revelation. Others, like me, have been forced upward — out of carnality and selfish living — through personal crises. Some have actually died — or come close to it — and returned like Lazarus from that marvelous place of peace to a world in turmoil.

All of us are confused about our dual status: one foot in heaven and the other on earth.

We all experience, as I am still experiencing, the problem of re-entry into "life as usual." We are different. Not like other people. We will always be that way. Having tasted from the sweet spring of intimacy with God, we will never again be satisfied with lapping from the earth's polluted puddles.

In Revelation 2:4-5 the risen Christ chided the pastor at Ephesus for having lost his first love. He told him: "Remember therefore from where you have fallen; repent and do the first works, or else I will come to you quickly and remove your lampstand from its place — unless you repent" (v. 5, NKJV).

We all need, on occasion, to stop and remember what our first love was like. We need to recall that overpowering rush of emotion that we now smile at and call puppy love.

I couldn't eat for thinking of her. I'd sneak away, find a phone and talk with her for hours about nothing. Those long nights, lying in bed looking at the ceiling — longing, dreaming. Oh, how I wanted to be with her. I'd rush off to school early to meet her in the parking lot. Just a smile, the touch of her hand, the smell of her perfume would set my heart beating wildly. Nothing mattered: father or mother, studies, sports — all faded into insignificance when I thought of her.

And I was only in the seventh grade.

So it is with those of us who have been to heaven's gate, have heard the sound of His voice, have felt the touch of His saving, healing hand. Nothing else — no love, no desire, no pleasure — will ever match His sweet, holy presence.

In 2 Corinthians 12:2, Paul described it as being "caught up to the third heaven." But to keep him from becoming conceited, God allowed a "thorn in the flesh" — a companion of pain — to accompany him on earth and be with him until his final return. Thorns, it seems, always accompany visits to glory. No one who has walked in His presence will ever be allowed to strut.

Don't regret the limp. Only fear that you lose that wonderful intimacy that came when life was so helpless and death so close.

Francis Frangipane once told me of the beginning of his little church in Cedar Rapids, Iowa. A spiritual idealist, he committed himself to spend every morning — all morning — in prayer. Then his church grew. (Churches with praying pastors always grow, it seems.) People with problems began to show up. There weren't enough hours in the day to minister to God and minister to people too. He cut his prayer time to three hours a day. Then two.

One day, he said, a young friend who had just spent the morning with God stopped by the house. He had a message from God.

"What did God say?"

"God said, 'Tell Francis I miss him.' "

Who among us, having tasted the sweet intimacy of walking with the Father, does not fear those sad words: "I miss you"?

The Bible emphasizes knowing God intimately as Father. As Daddy.

Jesus often used agricultural terms. Agriculture, in its most basic sense, is not learning how to control the seasons, soils and processes — it's learning how to cooperate with them.

So it is when you've walked with God. Instead of controlling time, you cooperate with time. Instead of controlling people, you cooperate with them. You love with the love of heaven — for you have been there.

Here's my prayer. You can pray it too.

"Lord, keep me aloft without being aloof. Show me how to remain in orbit with You above the earth's poisoned atmosphere, yet dipping at Your command to touch, instruct and heal as Jesus did. May I never again be 'of this world.' May I always — in my own mind and in the oft critical eyes of others — belong to a different kingdom. May I be in the world but not of the world, ministering at Your pleasure, marching ever to the sound of the different drummer."

Amen.

Sixty-seven

IT WILL
BE "NEAT"

L ITTLE APRIL'S question put me on the spot. She was five
years old and wanted me, her granddaddy, to tell her how
to get to heaven.

I told her you get there by dying. That didn't bother her. She's
not been taught you have to fear death. We were sitting at my
breakfast table, and I told her death was like a tunnel.

"Do I have to go through the tunnel alone?"

"No," I told her, "Jesus will hold your hand."

She thought that was "neat" and wanted to know when she
could go.

I told her that was God's business. All she had to do was be
ready — and stay close to Jesus.

That settled it for April. I only wish my faith was as strong.

It's not death that scares me. It's dying. Maybe I've watched
too much television. Maybe I've driven past too many wrecks on
the highway, been into too many morgues, walked through too
many refugee villages in Third World countries. Dying, from the
world's perspective, is not "neat."

I know this: The older I grow, the more determined I am to face
death victoriously.

Recently I found a note I wrote to myself several years ago, shortly after my eighty-seven-year-old daddy died. I was at a conference center in Green Lake, Wisconsin. That morning I had risen early and walked down to the lake. It was spring, and the crocuses and dogwoods were in full bloom. The sun was just rising over the mirrored surface of the lake. Two swans left a golden wake behind as they glided gracefully past. Everything spoke of life.

I sat on a bench and wrote.

"I wish I knew what happened that Sunday morning Daddy went to heaven. I've tried, to the best of my ability, to reconstruct all the events leading up to those last few moments. Mother has given, in detail, all she knew. What she didn't know, and what no one knows, was what went on in Daddy's mind.

"I think I know, but I'm so prone to wrongness, especially when it comes to knowing someone else's deepest thoughts, fears and desires. So it remains a great mystery — one upon which I can only speculate.

"There are times — like this morning, when I sit and get quiet in a strange place, apart from the madding crowd — that I wonder. And ask. I want to know, God. I want to know because I still love my daddy. I want to know because one day I will face the same transition. I learned so much from him. I want to learn of this, too.

"Was he afraid? I think not. He feared many things that were far less significant during his last months. He feared falling. He feared not having enough money to handle hospital bills. He feared leaving Mother alone and unattended. But I do not believe he feared dying. He had grown too close to God for that.

"Therefore, I believe when that Sunday came, and all the loose threads had been knotted and clipped, and suddenly he was helpless — unable to function physically — he laid his head on his pillow and willed himself into heaven.

"That's what I believe. Yet I want to know."

Dying, for my daddy, was "neat." He had walked long with the Lord. Like Enoch, he had come to the end of the day, and God said, "Walter, you're closer to My house than to yours. Come on home with Me." He did as old Jacob did. He "drew his feet up into the bed and breathed his last, and was gathered to his people" (Gen. 49:33b, NKJV).

My daddy, because of his childlike faith, did not fear dying. As

James Weldon Johnson, the black Southern poet, wrote of Sister Caroline in "Go Down, Death":

> She saw what we couldn't see;
> She saw Old Death.
> Coming like a falling star.
> But Death didn't frighten Sister Caroline;
> He looked to her like a welcome friend.

Mother called, and I arrived while his body was still warm; I wish I had been there when death took him home to Jesus.

Last week I visited my mother. She, too, has turned eighty-seven. She is just a few miles away in a cozy little apartment in the Baptist retirement center, located on the old homestead which was given by my father. Things are not well with her body. She has lost the ability to walk. She fears having to live out long years in bed. She was sitting there in the semidarkness trying to eat some clear soup, her spoon shaking and clattering against the side of the cup. Her once-exciting world has narrowed to four walls. She's not concerned about my travels or about the summit meetings in Geneva. Her big concern is getting to the bathroom in the middle of the night without falling.

"What do you want most?" I asked.

I thought she would say, "To come and live with you." In fact, I was hoping she would say that. Jackie and I had earlier agreed, knowing it would mean a radical shift in our life-style. But why not? She took care of me when I was a helpless child. Shouldn't I now care for her in her helplessness?

Instead she said, without pausing, "I want to go and be with Jesus. Now."

Well, why not? Her reason for living is to commune with God, and she can do that a lot better in heaven than here.

Jackie and I knelt beside her chair. I took her weak, wrinkled hands in mine — hands which once changed my diaper, which bathed and caressed me, which wiped away my tears — and I prayed, asking God to take her home. I asked God to dispatch His angel. "Go down, Death, and bring her to me."

I don't know when it will happen. I don't know how. But with April — and with Mother — I know this: It will be *neat*.

Sixty-eight

BRIDGE-BUILDERS

MOST OF my adult life, it seems, I've been trying to build bridges between people who don't want to come together. Last fall I got tired of the process and decided to build a real bridge — the kind made with timbers and nails.

For more than fifty years our family has owned a cabin on fifteen acres in the mountains of North Carolina. Behind the cabin, a sparkling little stream winds its way through the deep woods. We call it Brushy Branch.

Over the years three generations of Buckingham children have played in that wonderful stream. We've built dams, floated little boats, caught crawdads and even dug clay from its banks to make genuine Indian pottery.

Until last fall, however, no one had ever built a bridge. Instead, we used an old log, gingerly balancing as we crossed the stream. For years, every time I walked across that log, I dreamed of building a bridge. Last November I finally got around to it.

Using a broken yardstick taped together with masking tape and a length of hemp string, I measured the needed dimensions. I estimated it would take a sixteen-foot span, three feet wide and four feet above the ankle-deep water.

On a sheet of paper I sketched the diagram — the end posts, the braces, the spans, the planking, the side rail and the center posts that would have to be sunk in concrete in the streambed.

This was going to be a real bridge. Not a suspension bridge like the Golden Gate, nor an arch bridge like the Rainbow Bridge at Niagara Falls. It was going to be *my* bridge.

"Why not just put another log across the stream?" Jackie asked when I took her down to the building supply store and spent seventy dollars on pressure-treated lumber.

"You don't understand," I told her. "I've got to build this. Logs rot or wash away in the spring rains. This will be here many years after we're gone — providing safe passage for little feet across the dangerous narrows of Brushy Branch."

She smiled and seemed to understand. No one builds bridges for himself. Bridges are for those who follow after.

I had all the framework in place when my friend Bernie May arrived to spend a couple of days. For the last twelve years Bernie has been the U.S. director of Wycliffe Bible Translators. Under his leadership, Wycliffe has become one of the world's largest missionary organizations. The week before his visit to North Carolina, he had started the process of turning his job over to a younger man. It was time, he said, to seek the Lord for the even larger role he would play in making certain the Bible was translated into every language. Bernie May is one of the great bridge-builders in the kingdom.

"You're just in time," I told him when he arrived. "Change your clothes and come with me."

Giving him a hammer, I led him down the familiar wooded path to the site of the unfinished bridge. All that remained was to nail the forty-eight three-foot planks onto the spans. With Bernie straddling one span and me on the other, we started, nailing our way across the stream.

When we finished, Jackie joined us with a bag of roasted peanuts. We sat on the finished bridge, dangling our feet over the water, eating roasted peanuts and throwing the hulls into the flowing stream. Bernie said that was a time-honored tradition used by bridge-builders throughout the centuries. I think he made that up, but we did it anyway.

That night I slept soundly. Something seemed right. Complete. Maybe that's the sleep of all those who build bridges.

Since then I've thought a lot about some of the great bridge-builders.

When Billy Graham held his historic crusade in Montgomery, Alabama, in the sixties, he insisted on an integrated choir. The newspaper editorialized that Graham had come to Alabama and set the church back a hundred years. Graham's answer was classic: "If that's the case, I failed in my mission. I intended to set it back two thousand years." That's bridge building.

When David du Plessis attended Vatican II as a classic Pentecostal, he built bridges that many will use until Jesus comes.

In Chicago there is a brilliant young Orthodox rabbi, Yechiel Eckstein, who has spent most of his life helping his people understand Christians — and helping Christians understand Jews. Fierce opposition has come from both sides, yet he continues with his International Fellowship of Christians and Jews. In churches where he has spoken, he is widely acclaimed. Others sneer and call him an "unbeliever." Yet he is a true bridge-builder — and a dear friend.

There are thousands of other builders out there — carefully bridging chasms between people who are afraid to reach out to each other. Making sure little feet don't stumble.

There is no higher calling.

ABOUT THE EDITOR

LAURA WATSON worked closely with Jamie Buckingham for twenty years, doing the basic editing on most of his forty-seven books. Her most recent project was to prepare tapes and a workbook from the last writers' seminar that Jamie taught (*The Gift of Writing*, available from the Christian Writers' Institute).

Her task for this book was challenging — to select the best of Jamie's columns in *Charisma & Christian Life* magazine from the past thirteen years. Her choices reflect Jamie's unique perspective on issues he championed his entire life.

Laura and her husband, Brooks, live in Palm Bay, Florida, and have three children and eight grandchildren.

OTHER BOOKS BY JAMIE BUCKINGHAM
AVAILABLE FROM CREATION HOUSE

Let's Talk About Life

Parables

Summer of Miracles

Summer of Miracles Scripture cassette

The Truth Will Set You Free,
But First It Will Make You Miserable

For more information or to place an order, please contact:

Creation House
190 North Westmonte Drive
Altamonte Springs, FL 32714
1-800-451-4598